미얀마 투자 법규 · 세무 가이드

Legal & Tax Guide to Myanmar Foreign Investment

미얀마 투자 법규 · 세무 가이드

Legal & Tax Guide to Myanmar Foreign Investment

이용태 저

세창출판사

서 문
(미얀마 투자법제사)

산업 및 경제 개발의 중심은, 중세 이후 유럽본토에서 시작되어 영국을 거쳐, 대서양을 넘어 미국 동부, 서부를 가로질러, 다시 태평양을 건너 일본, 우리나라에 이어 중국, 베트남에 이른 근세 경제사의 "Going West" 바람은 이제 다시 새로운 기회의 땅을 찾아 동남아의 서쪽 해안에 자리한 미얀마로 밀려들고 있는 듯합니다.

이제 막 개방의 경제사를 시작한 미얀마(인구 5100만 명, 한반도의 3배 면적)는 최근 발족, 활성화되고 있는 ASEAN경제공동체(6.5억 명)의 중심에 있을 뿐만 아니라, 북쪽으로 중국(13.7억 명)과 방글라데시(1.7억 명), 서쪽으로 인도(12.5억 명), 동쪽으로 태국(6800만 명) 및 라오스(700만 명)와 국경을 접하고 있고 서쪽과 남쪽은 대양을 향해 길게 열려 있어, 지정학적으로 거대한 인접시장의 중심적 위치를 점하고 있어, 중국, 일본에 이어 2012년 이후 서방의 경제제재 완화와 개방에 따라 우리나라는 물론, 유럽 및 미국 등 서방 각국들로부터의 경제 원조 및 투자 경쟁이 뜨거워지고 있습니다.

특히, 2016년 4월 미얀마 민선2기이자 본격적인 민주정부 출범을 계기로 미얀마의 투자개방과 경제개발이 가속화될 것으로 전망됩니다. 이러한 시점에서, 정체된 국내경제 활성화와 중국-베트남에 이은 새로운 생산/제조기지의 대안으로 미얀마를 본격 검토하고 있는 우리 기업들에게 조그만 도움이라도 되길 바라는 마음에서 미얀마연방의 외국인 투자법규와 세무에 대한 실무안내서를 집필

하게 되었습니다.

1885년에서 1948년에 이르는 60년이 넘는 오랜 영국식민시기 동안,
- 현재까지도 유효하게 적용되고 있는 계약법(Contract Act of 1872), 회사법
  (Companies Act of 1914) 등 여러 기본법규들이 제정되었고,

1948년 영국으로부터 독립 후,
- 국가가 지분을 보유한 국영기업의 설립을 위해 특별회사법(Special Company
  Act of 1950)이 제정되었으며,

1962년 네윈의 군부 정권하에서 토지 등 주요 경제분야에 걸친 국유화와 계획
경제 등을 특징으로 하는 사회주의 경제체제하에서 자유시장경제와 고립되어
낙후되었던 버마는,
- 부동산 양도제한법(Transfer of Immovable Property Restriction Law of 1987)을 통
  해 외국인의 토지 소유 또는 임대를 제한하였고,

1988년 Union of Myanmar로 개명, (딴쉐 장군이 이끄는) 신군부 정권의 시장경
제 전환 및 대외 개방 선언과 함께
- 미얀마 외국인 투자법(Myanmar Foreign Investment Law of 1988)을 제정하며 외
  국인 투자유치 및 경제개발에 상당한 노력을 하였으나, 군부정권 내 강경파들
  의 득세에 따른 개방 후퇴, 인권탄압 및 비민주적 국정 운영에 따른 미국, 유럽
  등 서방으로부터의 경제제재 등으로 인해, 경제적 어려움을 겪게 되었습니다.

이후, 미얀마 신헌법(Union Constitution of 2008)에 따른 총선실시 후 2011년 3월,
신행정수도인 네피도에서 민선정부 출범 후(군부정권하 총리 역임한 군부 출신인
떼인쉐인이 대통령으로 선출),
- 2011년 한 해만도 15개에 달하는 주요 경제관련 입법을 시행하고,
- 2012년 11월, 외국인 투자법 개정(Foreign Investment Law of 2012) 및 2013년 국
  가계획경제개발부의 외국인 투자법 시행령(MNPED Notification 1/2013), 2014년

특별경제구역법(Special Economic Zone Law of 2014) 및 이후 현재까지 매년 지속된 미얀마 투자위원회 시행령 및 고시를 통한 투자 인센티브 확대 및 외국인 투자 제한 완화,

- 2012년 시행된 외환관리법(Foreign Exchange Management Law, FEML, 2012)과 시장환율 제도 도입(2012.4월),
- 2014년, 2015년 및 2016년 연방세법(Union Tax Law)에 이르기까지 매년 세제 개선을 통해 내외국인 세금 차별을 철폐,
- 2013년 7월, 외국중재판정의 효력 인정과 집행에 관한 뉴욕협약(the New York Convention on the Recognition and Enforcement of Foreign Arbitral Awards: "뉴욕협약") 인준에 이어 이를 이행할 새로운 중재법[Arbitration Law of 2016"(Union Law 5/2016; 신 중재법)]을 시행하는 등,

투자 보호 및 송금보장 등 투자환경 개선을 통한 적극적인 외국인 투자유치와 개방경제 정책을 강력히 추진한 결과, 2013년 미국, 유럽 등 서방국가들의 대미얀마 경제제재도 사실상 철회되었고, 2013년부터 현재까지 연평균 GDP성장률 8%대의 가시적인 경제성장 효과를 거두고 있습니다.

절대 다수 국민의 개혁과 인권, 경제개발 가속화에 대한 열의에 힘입어, 2015년 11월 총선결과, 2016년 4월 출범한 민선2기 신정부[아웅산 수지 여사가 이끄는 NLD(National League for Democracy)당이 집권, 헌법상 제한으로 측근인 틴쩌가 대통령으로 취임]에 대한 대내외적 관심과 지지에 힘입어 외국인 투자유치 촉진과 개방을 통한 경제개발이 더욱 가속화될 것으로 전망되고 있으나, 현정부의 중점 정책과제인 민주화, 인권/노동권익 보호 및 소수민족과의 화합을 통한 국가통합(미얀마는 135개의 민족으로 구성) 등 추진과정에서 외국자본 유치 및 경제개발 정책과의 충돌로 인한 지체 또는 후퇴 위험성도 간과할 수 없습니다.

민선 1기 정부 말에 초안이 완성되어, 현 정부에 넘겨져 의회상정을 위해 검토 중인 주요 외국인 투자관련 개정법안으로는,
- 식민시기에 제정된 구시대적 회사법에 대한 전면 개정안(현대의 시대적 요구에

부합한 투명하고 일관성 있는 준법경영 및 회계관리 의무를 기업에 부과하여 미얀마 경제의 견실성 강화 목적)
- 미얀마 시민 투자법(Myanmar Citizen Investment Law of 2013)과 외국인 투자법(Foreign Investment Law of 2012)의 통합입법안(형평과 일관성을 유지한 모범적 입법사례 정립을 통해, ASEAN 경제공동체 확립의 초석을 이루고자 하는 의지 표명 목적)
- 지적재산권 관련 4대 입법안(특허권, 산업디자인권, 저작권, 상표권) 등이 있습니다.

이상, 살펴본 바와 같이,
현재까지 적용되고 있는 미얀마의 투자 관련 법규는 역사상 영국식민지 시기에서 시작하여 현재에 이르기까지 상이한 시대적, 정치적 배경을 가진 다양한 법규들로 구성되어 있습니다.

즉, 제정 시기별로 영미법제와 대륙법제가 혼재되어 있고, 대부분의 기본법들은 식민시기에 제정되어 성문법적 기초가 약한 반면,

그 이후 법문화 및 판례 발전이 미흡하여 해석상 상당한 어려움이 있으며, 상대적으로 최근에 제/개정된 외국인 투자 관련 법규나 세법 등의 경우에도, 기본법보다는 시행령과 고시를 통해 해마다 빠르게 수정, 변화하고 있는 반면, 상당수 법규가 모호하게 서술되어 명확한 해석이 어려워, 담당관에 따른 자의적인 보충해석이 개입될 여지가 많습니다.

또한, 입법예고나 체계적인 사전 공고/고시 시스템이 갖춰져 있지 않고, 아직도 폐쇄적인 정부부처의 정보/문화 환경 및 열악한 인터넷, DB환경 등으로 인해 일반대중들이 이러한 법령 정보에 접근하는 것이 원만치 않음은 물론, 외국인의 입장에서는, 그나마도 법령/고시 등의 영문화 작업 및 공개 속도가 느려, 최신 관련 법규 정보의 확인 및 이해에는 상당한 어려움이 있습니다.

필자의 경우, 미얀마 국가기획경제개발부의 법률고문으로서 정부 깊숙이 들어와 있다는 이점을 내세워, 미얀마어 원문 법령 수집, 번역 및 관련 부처 방문, 면

담 등을 통해 최근 개정현황 및 내용의 정확성 재확인 등의 작업과정을 거쳤음에도, 적지 않은 오류나 미처 따라잡지 못한 일부 update 미비 등의 발생 가능성을 배제할 수 없음에 대해 독자 여러분의 너그러운 양해를 미리 구함과 동시에, 향후 정기적인 update 작업을 통해, 상황에 따라 on-line 또는 off-line상으로 최신 개정내용을 제공할 것을 약속드립니다.

축복은 내려지는 것이 아니라,
올바르게 생활하는 가운데 나타나는 것이라는
가르침을 되새기며,

2016년 6월
이 용 태

차 례

참고 문헌

2014 투자유망국 비교포럼, KOTRA, 2014.12.11.

미얀마 투자법제, 법무부, 2013.

미얀마 투자실무 가이드, KOTRA, 2013.

A Critical First look at Myanmar's New Arbitration Law, Client Briefing Note, VDB/Loi, 2016.

Burma Investment Climate Statement 2015, US Department of State, May 2015.

Doing Business In Myanmar, BNG Legal, June 2014.

Doing Business In Myanmar, Myanmar Legal Services Ltd., May 2016.

How To Register Your Company In Myanmar (Handbook), DICA, Dec. 2015.

Labour Law Seminar Summry Report, Law Plus Ltd., Dember 2015.

Legal, Tax & Investment Guide: Myanmar, DFDL, 2014.

Myanmar Business Guide, pwc, 3rd edition, July 2015.

Myanmar Investment Guidelines, DICA(투자회사관리청), 2016.

Myanmar－a new law for a new era, Global Arbitration Review, Law Busienss Reserch Ltd., Feb. 2016.

OECD Investment Policy Reviews: Myanmar 2014, OECD.

Tax Pocket Guide To Investment In Myanmar, DFDL, 2015.

Union Tax Law 2016, Myanmar Tax Alert, KPMG, 2016.

I. 외국인 투자 사업 유형
Forms of Business

A. 외국인 투자 방식

외국인 투자법 및 동 시행령[MNPED(경제기획개발부) Notification 11/2013]상, 외국인은 아래와 같은 3가지 유형으로 투자를 할 수 있다.

1. 외국인 단독투자 법인[Wholly(100%) Foreign-Owned Entity]

외국인 투자자가 미얀마에서의 사업영위를 위하여 미얀마 상법에 따라 단독으로 회사, 지점 또는 연락사무소 등을 설립, 운영하는 방법

2. 합작(Joint Venture)

외국인 투자자와 미얀마 현지 파트너 간의 합작형태로 사업을 영위하는 방법에는:

(a) 합작법인을 설립, 운영하는 합작 투자(Equity JV)와
(b) 별도 합작법인 설립 없이 파트너들 간의 계약상의 합작(Contractual JV)을 통해 특정사업을 공동수행하는 방법이 있다.

미얀마 회사법상, 합작기업에 대한 외국인 지분 최소 또는 최대 제한 요건은 없으나, 외국인 투자법상 합작기업의 형태로만 외국인 투자참여가 허용되는 사업영역에 대해서는 외국인 지분 최고한도가 80%까지로 제한된다.

3. 기타 협력계약(Contractual Arrangement)

외국인 투자자와 현지 파트너들 간의 아래와 같은 사업협력 계약관계 구성을 통해 목적하는 사업을 추진하는 것도 가능하다.

(a) 대리점 또는 판매점 계약(Agency or Distribution)

(b) 조합 또는 전략제휴 계약(Partnership or other Strategic Alliances)

(c) 부동산 개발업 등의 경우처럼, BOT[Build-Operate-Transfer: 사업운영권자가 건설(설립)하여, 계약기간동안 운영 후, 계약만료시점에 관계당국에 사업을 이전하는 모델] 계약, BTO[Build-Transfer-Operate: 사업운영권자가 건설(설립)하여, 사업을 관계당국에게 이전한 후, 계약기간동안 사업운영권자가 사업을 운영하는 모델] 계약 또는 프로젝트 파이낸싱과 EPC 계약(Engineering, Procurement & Construction: 설계, 구매, 건설 통합계약 또는 Turn-key 계약) 등과 같은 다양한 계약관계를 구성하여 외국인 투자자를 포함한 민간 및 정부기관 간의 협력을 통해 사업을 수행하는 형태

B. 투자 법인 형태

1. 유한책임회사(Limited Liability Company)

미얀마 회사법상, 유한책임회사는 대부분 국가의 주식회사와 유사한 개념과 특징을 가지고 있고, 미국이나 유럽 법제와는 달리, 주식회사와는 다른 별도 유형의 유한회사[1]가 존재하지 않는다. 미얀마에서의 조합(Partnership)은 유한책임회사와 비교하여 세무 등 관점에서 실익이 없고, 투자자에게 무한책임이 부과되는 관계로, 거의 대부분의 내국 및 외국인 기업들이 유한책임회사의 형태로 설립, 운영되고 있다.

---

1 미국이나 유럽 법제상 유한회사(limited liability company)의 경우, 주식회사와는 달리, 조합의 경우처럼, 소득세 과세 대상이 유한회사가 아닌 투자주이며, 유한회사의 손익이 각 투자자에게 지분율 또는 기타 합의율로 이양되어(pass through) 분리 과세되는 특성을 가짐.

즉, 조합(Partnership)의 경우에도 조합 자체가 직접 과세 대상이므로, 조합의 영업이익이 조합원의 지분 등에 따라 조합원에게 분배/배정되고 각 조합원이 이에 따른 소득세를 부담하는 방식이 아니며,

조합뿐만 아니라 유한책임회사에도 이익배당의 근원이 된 수익에 대해 해당 법인에 소득세가 부과되었다면, 별도의 이익배당세가 주주에게 부과되지 않으므로, 주주에 대한 이익배당세 부과에 따른 이중과세 부담이 없다는 점에서도 조합과 동일한 효과를 거둘 수 있는 반면,

미얀마 조합법(Partnership Act of 1932)상, 모든 조합은 조합원이 무한 책임의무를 부담하며, 유한책임 형태로 구성이 불가하여, 모든 조합원이 무한 책임을 부담하여야 하는 리스크가 있으므로(우리법상 합명회사와 유사), 유한책임회사 보다 오히려 불리한 책임구조를 갖게 되므로, 법인의 책임이나 세무 부담 측면에서 오히려 불리한 조합보다는 유한책임회사의 형태로 설립, 운영하고 있다. 조합의 경우도, 회사 등록이 가능하나 의무는 아니다.

미얀마 회사법상 유한 책임회사는
  (a) 비공개 유한책임회사(private limited liability company)와
  (b) 공개 유한책임회사(public limited liability company)의 두 종류가 있다.

비공개 유한책임회사(우리법상 유한회사와 유사)의 경우는 주식의 이전, 양도가 제한되는 관계로 일반대중들을 상대로 한 주식의 일반공모가 불가하고, 주주의 수는 최소 2명 이상 최고 50명으로 제한된다. 2016년 4월말 현재까지 외국인 투자회사는 모두 비공개 유한책임회사이며 공개회사의 형태로 설립된 예가 없다.

공개 유한책임회사는 공개시장에서 일반대중을 대상으로 주식 발행, 공모를 할 수 있으며, 최소 7명의 주주를 필요로 한다.

유한책임회사에 적용되는 준거법은 1914년에 제정된 미얀마 회사법(Companies

Act of 1914)으로 회사법에 따르면, 외국인 투자기업은 법인형태(단독투자기업, 합작투자기업, 지점 또는 연락사무소)와 상관없이 영업허가(Permit to Trade)와 법인등록(Company Registration Certificate)을 필수 요건으로 한다. 단, 국영자본(State Equity)과의 합작기업의 경우는, 회사법상 등록 규정이 아니라, 국영기업에 대한 적용법규인 미얀마 특별회사법(Company Act of 1950)에 따라 등록하여야 하며, 특별법상 적용배제에 대한 명시적 조항이 없는 한, 회사법상 기타 제반 조항들은 특별회사에도 적용되게 된다.

2. 지점(Branch of a foreign company)

본사를 대리하여 제한적인 범위 내에서 영리활동 가능하고, 외국회사의 지점은 본사의 사무실로 간주되므로 본사가 지점에 대한 종국적인 책임을 부담하게 된다.

3. 연락사무소(Representative office of foreign company)

현지와 본사 간의 연락 및 본사에서 필요한 데이터나 정보 수집, 홍보 등의 비영리 업무를 수행할 수 있으나, 직접적인 영업활동이나 수익창출 활동을 할 수는 없다.

II. 외국인 투자 절차
Foreign Investment Procedures

A. 외국인 투자법(Foreign Investment Law)

외국인 투자자가 미얀마에서 회사를 설립하여 사업을 하고자 하는 경우, 외국인 투자법에 따라:

(i) 미얀마 투자위원회(Myanmar Investment Committee)의 투자허가(MIC Permit)

(ii) 투자회사관리국(DICA: Directorate of Investment & Company Administration)의 영업허가(Permit to Trade[1])와 함께

(iii) 회사등록사무소(DICA 산하기관)에 등록(Company Registration)하는 절차를 경유하여야 한다.

현재 상기 3개 허가/등록 절차는 DICA의 본점(양곤)에 소재한 종합서비스센터(One Stop Service Center)에서 일괄적으로 신청, 진행할 수 있으며, 특히, (ii) 영업허가(Permit to Trade)는 별도의 신청양식이나 절차 없이 (iii)의 신청절차에 포함되어 일괄적으로 진행된다.

---

1 Permit to Trade라는 공식영문표기로 인해, 일부 문헌에서 무역 또는 수출입 허가로 오해 또는 오역하는 경우가 있으나, 미얀마 회사법상 Permit to Trade는 business license, 즉 영업 또는 사업허가로 이해하여야 하고, 상무부 무역국에서 관장하는 수출입 허가(현재는 폐지)나 수출입업체 등록과는 다른 허가임을 유의 바람.

물론, 외국인 투자법상 투자허가 절차 없이, 일반 회사법상 절차에 따라 (ii) 영업허가와 (iii) 회사등록 절차를 통해 사업을 진행할 수도 있으나, 이 경우 외국인 투자법규상의 세금 감면 등 투자 인센티브를 받을 수 없으므로 대부분의 경우는 외국인 투자법상 투자허가를 거쳐 회사를 등록하고 사업을 진행하고 있다.

단, DICA 행정실무상, (a) 호텔업, (b) 10층 이상 건물 건설 및 (c) 제조업 공장의 경우에는 반드시 MIC 투자허가신청을 경유하여야 하며, MIC 허가 신청 없이, 회사법상 영업허가와 회사등록 신청만 하는 경우에는 접수가 거절됨을 유의 바란다(DICA 방문, 실무 간부 면담 통해 확인한 사항).

실무상, DICA의 종합지원서비스센터를 통한 세무, 노동, 비자, 환경관련 인허가신청 등 종합 민원 혜택은 MIC 투자신청기업을 대상으로 이루어지고 있고, MIC 투자허가 신청이 병행되지 않은 회사 등록신청의 경우에는 해당 영업허가와 회사등록 신청만 접수, 관리하고 그 외 행정 지원은 제공되지 않는다.

[참고]

미얀마 투자위원회(MIC: Myanmar Investment Committee)는 외국인 투자법과 시민 투자법을 집행하는 기관으로 조직되었으며, 외국인 투자에 대한 승인 및 투자관리, 감독기관으로, *2016년 3월말 기준* 관련 정부부처 장관급 인사 6명, 민간인사 5명 등 총 11명으로 구성되어 있고, 현재 외국인 투자업무와 관련하여 MIC의 상위기관은 없다.

MIC는 일종의 회의체인 관계로, 국가기획경제개발부(Ministry of National Planning & Economic Development, 2016년 4월 신정부 출범에 따라 현재 Ministry of Panning & Finance로 통합 재편) 산하 투자기업국(DICA: Directorate of Investment & Company Administration)에서 MIC의 사무국 역할을 맡아 대부분의 행정업무를 수행하고 있다. DICA는 외국인 투자는 물론 내국인 투자의 경우에도 요구되는, 회사법에 따른 모든 법인의 영업 허가, 등록 및 관리 행정업무를 관장하며, 법인 등록 및 관리 업무를 위해 산하에 **회사 등록청**(Company Registration Office)을 두고 있다.

외국인 투자 유치 촉진과 외국인 투자자 편의제공을 위해 DICA에 총 14개 관련 정부 기관(DICA, 상무부, 재무부(국세청 및 관세청), 이민부, 노동부, 산업부, 산업행정/검사부, 전력부, 중앙은행, 광산부, 농업부, 축산/수산부, 산림/환경부, 호텔/관광부)으로부터 파견된 담당관으로 구성된 범정부 합동팀 형태의 **통합투자지원센터**(OSS, One Stop Service Center for Investment and Company Registration)를 DICA의 본점 사무소(No.1, Thitsar Road, Yankin Township, Yangon) 내에 설립(2013.4.10), 운영하고 있고, 이를 통해 MIC 투자허가 신청을 하는 외국인 투자자를 대상으로 투자 허가, 영업허가, 회사등록은 물론 수출입업자 등록, 세무/통관 신고, 비자 및 취업허가, 노동 신고, 전력공급 신청, 환경관련 평가/허가 및 해당 산업관련 필요한 인허가, 외화 반입/송금, 국내 산업 및 투자관련 자문 등 외국인 투자관련 모든 행정 편의를 제공하고 있다.

MIC 투자 허가, 영업허가 및 회사등록 등의 절차, 신청 서류 및 관련 비용 등 상
세 내용은 아래 요약표와 같다.

* DICA 실무절차 지침상 기준(2016. 5월)에 따름
* Ks(짯): 미얀마 현지화폐로 2016.5.10. 기준 US$1 = 1,168Ks, KRW 1원 = 1Ks

	절차 및 서류	기간 및 비용	비고
A. 투자허가 (MIC Permit) [신청기관] 미얀마 투자위원회 (MIC)	외국인 투자자는 외국인 투자법 및 시행령상 절차규정에 따라, Proposal Form (1) 양식에 따른 투자제안서를 작성하여 아래 서류와 함께 MIC에 제출하여야 한다. [부록 3. 참조] 1. 투자자 신분 증빙: (회사인 경우) 회사등록증명서(사본) 2. (개인인 경우): 신분증(사본) 및 여권(사본) 3. 투자자의 경제적 타당성을 보여줄 재무 및 영업 현황관련 증빙자료 4. 합작계약서(초안) 및 (정부기관과의 계약인 경우) 법무장관실 추천서 5. 정관 및 회사 규정 6. 토지위치도 및 토지소유권 증명서 7. 토지임차계약서(초안) 및 정부기관과의 계약인 경우, 법무장관실 추천서 8. 종업원 고용계획서(현지인 및 외국인) 9. 종업원 사회보장 및 복지 계획서 10. 환경영향평가(Environmental Impact Assessment) 11. 사회경제영향평가(Social	1. 투자제안서 및 필요 서류 접수 * 접수비: 5,000Ks(투자제안서 양식은 DICA사무소 현장에서 입수 또는 웹사이트 통한 다운로드 가능) 2. MIC는 투자제안서 접수 후 15일 내에, (기초심사) 제안서류 검토를 통해, 투자심사진행 또는 심사 거절여부를 결정, 통보한다. 3. 심사진행 결정시, (본안심사) MIC는 제안서 접수일로부터 90일 이내에 투자허가 여부를 결정한다.	• 외국인 투자자는 MIC 투자허가 없이 바로 회사법상 등록절차를 거쳐 사업을 시작할 수 있으나, MIC 투자허가 받은 회사와는 달리 외국인투자법상 세금 및 기타 투자인센티브 혜택을 받을 수 없음. • 단, 현재 DICA 실무상, (i) 호텔, (ii) 10층 이상 건물의 건축 및 (iii) 생산 공장의 경우에는 MIC 투자허가 신청 없이 회사법상 회사등록만 신청시 접수가 거절된다. • MIC 심사 평가기준: - 외국인투자법상 정책과의 부합성 - 재무적 신뢰도 - 경제적 견실성 및 현행 법규 부합성 * 경우에 따라, MIC는, 투자허가 후에도, 투자자에게, 외국인투자법에 따라 관련 투자 계약상 조건을 수정할 수 있도록 허가할 수 있다. 투자자

	Economic Impact Assessment)		가, MIC투자허가를 받은 회사의 주식을 양도하고 자 하는 경우에는, 종전 에 받았던 투자허가를 포 기하고, MIC의 사전허가 를 받아야 한다.
B. 영업허가 Permit to Trade [신청기관] DICA	• 현행 DICA실무 지침에 따르면, 별도의 절차나 추가적인 신청서 류 없이, 회사등록 신청 절차에 포함되어 일괄 진행됨. [신청서 양식(Form A), 부록 4 참 조]	• 영업허가 유효기간: 허가일로부터 5년 (갱신 가능)	• 회사법상, 외국기업 (단 1명의 외국인 주주 가 있는 경우에도 외국 인회사로 분류됨)의 경 우에는 국가기획개발부 (현재 기획재정부)로 부 터 영업허가를 받아야 한다. 단, 정부 또는 국 영기업이 주주로 참여 하거나 기타 특별회사 법에 따라 설립된 국영 기업과의 합작회사의 경우에는 영업허가 요 건이 적용되지 않는다.
C. 회사등록 Company Registration [신청기관] CRO	[STEP 1] 회사명 점검 신청서(DICA 고유양 식, 부록 4 참조) 기재 및 서명후 DICA에 제출(신청한 회사명이 기 존 회사명과 중복되는지 여부 점 검 목적) [STEP2] 회사등록양식(Company Registration Forms)과 함께 아래 부속서류 첨부하여 DICA에 제출 [부록 4 참조] [외국인 회사 등록 신청 필요서류] 1. 신청서 표지서한 (Application cover letter) 2. 등록선언서(Declaration of	① 사명점검신청서 접수비: 1,000Ks, 양식은 DICA사무소 현 장 입수 또는 웹사이트 통해 다운로드 가능 ② 회사등록 신청서 접 수비(5,100Ks, 양식은 DICA 현장 또는 웹사 이트 다운로드) ③ 인지대(Stamp duty) 납부, (종합서 비스센터 또는 관할 세무당국에 납부) : (인지대 금액: 승인자본 금에 따라 65,000 Ks~ 165,000 Ks) * 협회(Associations)는	• 일반적으로 MIC투자 허가신청과 회사등록신 청은 동시에 제출, 접수 하고 있음. • 외국인 투자법상, 최 소자본요건규정은 없고, 투자제안서상 투자계획 에 따라, 해당 자본금을 미얀마로 송금, 투자하 도록 하고 있으나, 은행 및 보험업의 경우는 미얀 마 중앙은행 규정에 따른 최소자본 요건을 충족하 여야 함. ® 회사법상 제 조업 회사의 경우 USD 150,000, 서비스업 회사 의 경우는 USD 50,000

registration, Form 1)
3. 등록사무소 위치확인서 (Situation of registered office form)
4. 법적 서류 선언서(Declaration of Legal Version)
5. 번역증명서(Certificate of Translation)
6. 회사 영업범위 기술 및 무역업 금지 확약서(Statement of company objectives and undertaking not to conduct trading)
7. 이사진 관련 상세 정보 (Form 26)
8. 정관(Memorandum of Association)
9. 회사규정(Articles of Association)
10. 영업허가신청서(Application form for permit; Form A)
11. 주주 여권 사본(개인주주인 경우) 또는 이사회 의결서(회사가 주주인 경우)
12. 외국인 이사 여권 사본 및 내국인 이사 신분증(National Registration Card)

[외국인 지점 및 연락사무소 경우]
상기 서류 외에 아래 서류 추가 필요
- 본사 정관 및 회사규정 또는 본사 설립 증명 서류(본사 설립지 소재 미얀마 대사관의 공증 필요)
- 최근 2년간 재무제표 또는 대차대조표 및 손익계산서(본사설립지 소재 미얀마 대사관 공증 필요)
- (정관 및 회사설립 증명서류가

인지대 면제
④ 등록비 납부—비공개회사(Private LLC): 500,000Ks, 공개회사(Public LLC): 2,500,000Ks (2016.6.1 변경)

로 최소 자본금 요건 규정
• 그러나 DICA 실무지침상, MIC 투자허가 신청한 외국회사, 지점, 연락사무소의 경우 US$150,000, 기타 회사의 경우는 US$50,000의 최소자본금을 등록 허가 요건으로 하며, 이 실무지침상 요건은 외국인 기업에만 적용되며, 현지기업에는 적용되지 않음.
• 상기 최초자본금의 50% 이상이 미얀마 은행으로 송금, 납입된 은행 예금증명서가 회사 등록시까지 제출되어야 하며, 나머지 50%는 회사등록 유효기간인 5년 이내에 국내로 송금, 납입되어야 한다. (DICA실무상 잔여 50% 자본금 납입확인 시점은 유효기간경과에 따른 갱신 신청시에 이루어진다)
• 비공개 회사는 회사설립증명서 발급후 영업을 개시할 수 있으나, 공개회사의 경우에는 영업개시 전에 반드시 별도의 영업개시증명서(Certificate of Commencement of Business)를 신청(관할관청: DICA)하여야 한다.

	영어로 작성되지 않은 경우) 원문 및 영어번역 인증본 [STEP 3] (선택사항) 임시 설립증명서 및 임시영업허가증 발급 (발급기관: DICA; 유효기간: 6개월) [STEP 4] (i) 초기자본 납입 증명서, (ii) 추가 조건 서약서(Permit Conditions Letter) 서명본 및 (iii) 등록사무소 주소 확인서(관할 행정기관 발급) 제출 [STEP 5] 최종 등록증(Permanent Registration Certificate) 및 영업허가증(Permanent Permit) 발급 (유효기간: 5년, 갱신가능)	* 임시 등록증 교부기간은 등록신청 접수완료 후 3일 이내이나, 최종 등록증 발급기간에는 제한이 없으므로, 신청자가 승인된 최초자본금의 50% 납입증명 등 등록에 필요한 요건을 완료할 때까지 등록을 보류할 수 있다.	
D. 상업세 등록 Commercial Tax Registration [관할지역 세무당국]	상업세 부과 대상 매출이 예상되는 영업개시 전 1개월 이내에 해당 회사 관할 세무당국(Township IRD)에 등록하여야 하며, 영업개시 후 10일 이내에 관할 세무당국에 영업개시 사실을 통보하여야 함.		
E. 수출입 등록 Exporter/ Importer Registration [담당기관] (상무부) 무역국	• 수출입업자 등록 양식 • 회사등록 증명서 및 DICA 발급 서신 • Form 6(주식 배정/양도 현황) • Form 26(이사진 현황) • 이사진 사진 및 서명 샘플 • 정관 및 규정 원본 • 위임장 (대리인 신청시)	* 1년: 50,000Ks * 2년: 100,000Ks * 갱신시에도 동일 수수료	• 현재까지 외국계 무역법인의 투자를 허용하지 않고 있어, 실무상 (제조업 없이) 순수 무역업만을 위한 외국인 투자법인 설립은 허용되지 않고 있음.

	* 수출입관리법[Control of Imports & Exports (temporary) Act of 1947]에 의해 규율 * 한 번의 등록으로 수출업과 수입업 모두 가능 * 외국인 투자법상 설립된 제조업체(외국인 단독 또는 합작 회사, 조합, 외국기업 지사 등) 가 수출 또는 수입을 하기 위해서는 수출입업자로 등록하여야 한다. 단, 과거에 존재하던 개별 수출입건마다 일괄적으로 요구된 사전 수출허가 또는 수입허가 제도는 폐지되었으나(2013.3), 아직도 상당수 제품은 개별적 수출입 허가를 필요로 함(상무부 고시를 통해 허가 면제품목 확대 추세임).		
F. 외국인회사 운영요건	a. 주식 배정시마다 1개월 이내 DICA에 등록 date b. 이사, 경영진 등 주요 관리자 등록 및 변경 통보(선임 또는 변경후 14일 이내) c. 공식문건 수발신 및 통지목적상 등록사무소 주소 등 정보 통지(회사등록시 및 이후 변경시 28일 이내) d. (설립직후) 외부감사 선임 e. 창립주주총회(설립후 18개월 이내) 및 이후 정기 주주총회(매년 1회, 이전 주총후 15개월 이내 개최) f. 주총관련 서류 제출/통보 의무(해당 주총후 21일 이내) : 　① 이사 및 주주 명부 　(List of members & directors) 　② 상세 자본 구조 현황 　(Details of capital structure) 　③ 회사자산에 대한 담보설정		• 재무제표는 국제회계표준위원회가 설정한 국제재무보고기준 및 국제회계기준(International Financial Reporting Standards and International Accounting Standards)에 기초한 미얀마 회계기준(Myanmar Accounting Standards)을 준수하여 작성하여야 함 • 또한, 미얀마 공인회계사가 감사한 재무제표와 함께 매년 세무신고서를 관할 세무당국에 제출하여야 한다. • 회계/재무자료상 법정화폐는 미얀마 현지화폐(짯, Ks)로 표기.

	현황(Details of mortgages over company property) ④ 일반대중에 대한 주식 공개 공모/배정 사실이 없음을 확약 하는 증명서 g. 특별 주총 소집 사전통보(15일 전) 및 특별주총 의결서(의결후 15일내) 제출/통보 h. 회계장부 및 법정 요건 문서 보관의무(주주 및 이사 등록부, 주식 발행/배정, 담보 및 기타 저 당/질권 설정 현황 등 i. 매회계연도별 감사필한 재무제 표를 주총에 제출/보고할 의무 j. (외국회사 지점 및 연락사무소 경우) 매년 본사의 재무제표 및 주총 보고서 제출의무		
G. 회사등록 갱신 Renewal of Company Registration Certificate	외국인 회사기준 필요서류: ● 등록갱신 신청서(Application for renewal of registration), ● 영업허가 신청서(Form A), 기입 완료 및 서명본 2부 ● 상세 영업활동 목록(detailed list of the company's business activities) ● 이사 및 주주 명부(list of directors/shareholders), ● Form E, 기재완료 및 서명본 ● 최근 2년간(감사필) 재무제표 (Audited financial statements for the last two years), ● 납입자본관련 신용조언(Credit advices) ● MIC 허가(permit) 사본 ● (관광업 경우) 관광업체 라이선 스 및 호텔/관광부에 제출한 월간 보고서 ● 세무신고서(확인 필증) 사본	갱신등록비 : 300,000Ks (2016.6.1 변경)	● 갱신등록증 유효기 간: 5년(국내외 기업, 지점, 연락사무소 및 비 영리단체 공통) ● 모든 법인은 법인 등 록 만료일 전에 반드시 등록증 갱신하여야 함.

B. 특별경제구역법(Special Economic Zone Law)

외국인 투자자는 외국인 투자법에 따른 투자외에, 정부가 승인한 특별경제구역 내에 투자하고자 하는 경우는 특별경제구역법(Special Economic Zone Law of 2014)에 따른 투자도 가능하다. 단, 특별경제구역 내 투자에 대해서는 외국인 투자법은 적용되지 않는다.

● 현재까지 공표된 5대 특구는, Dawei 특별경제구역(남부), Kyaukphyu 경제기술 구역(서부), Thilawa 항만 특별경제구역(양곤 인근), Kokang 특구(샨주), Myawaddy 특구(카렌주)이고, 이중 Thilawa, Dawei, Kyankphyu 등 3대 특구는 운영을 개시하였다.

● 2014년 개정된 특별경제구역법은 2011년 제정된 특별경제구역법(Special Economic Zone Law of 2011)과 Dawei 특별경제구역법(2011)을 폐지하고 대체된 전면 개정 법규이다.

● 특별경제구역법에 따른 투자의 경우는, MIC가 아니라 2011년 4월 대통령실을 통해 조직된 특별경제구역중앙관리청(Central Body for Myanmar Sepcial Economic)이 관할당국으로 해당 투자의 승인 · 관리 등을 총괄하되, 각 특별경제구역별 투자허가 신청 승인 및 세부적인 운영은 물론 SEZ법규하의 세부시행령 및 규칙 등도 해당 특별경제구역별 운영위원회(management committee)가 담당하고 있다. 특별경제구역 내 투자에 대한 모든 투자허가, 회사등록 등 영업에 필요한 제반 인허가, 등록 절차는 해당 특구 운영위원회가 운영하는 one stop service center 를 통해 이루어지므로, 기타 다른 정부기관을 별도로 접촉할 필요가 없다. (Thilawa 특별 경제구역 운영위원회 참조: http://www.myanmarthilawa.gov.mm/)

● 이러한 특별경제구역별 개별 승인 및 관리 시스템을 통해 투자신청일로부터 30일 이내 승인여부를 결정하도록 운영하고 있다(외국인 투자법상 MIC 투자허가 프로세스상 90일 기준 대비, 대폭 단축).

- 특별경제구역법은,

  세부 지역별로,

    i) 면제지구(Exempted Zone), ii) 진흥지구(Promotion Zone) 및 iii) 기타 지구로,

  투자업종도,

    i) 면제지구 업종(Exempted zone business)과 ii) 기타 업종으로,

  투자자도,

    i) 개발업자(developer)와 ii) 사업 투자자(investor)로 구분하여,

  각 해당 유형에 따라 다른 요건과 인센티브를 적용하고 있다. 면제지구 투자자로 등록되기 위해서는 생산액의 75% 이상 수출 요건을 충족하여야 하며, 수출용 생산업체를 지원하는 물류업체도 면제지구 회사로 등록될 수 있다. 그 외 내수용 생산업체는 진흥지구 회사로 등록할 수 있다.

- 아직까지, 외국인 투자법규 및 시행령과는 달리, 특별경제구역법에 따른 후속 시행령 등이 발표되지 않아 세부 기준이나 절차 등이 미흡한 상황이다.

III. 외국인 투자 제한
Foreign Investment Restrictions

A. 국영기업 독점사업(민간기업 사업금지) 영역

국영기업법(State-Owned Economic Enterprises Law of 1989, No. 9/89, 제 II.1조)은 연방정부만이 운영할 수 있는 12개 독점사업을 아래와 같이 지정하고 있어, 이러한 국영기업 독점영역에 대해서는 원칙적으로 외국인 또는 외국인 기업뿐만 아니라, 미얀마 시민이나 내국 법인도 사업참여가 금지된다.

1. 티크목 벌채 및 국내외 판매
2. 숲 경작 및 보존 (단, 주민들의 개인적 소비를 위한 마을소유 땔감 경작은 예외적으로 허용)
3. 원유 및 천연가스 탐사, 채굴, 생산 및 판매
4. 진주, 옥 및 기타 보석류 탐사, 채굴 및 수출
5. 정부가 연구용도로 보존한 (양)어장에서의 물고기 및 새우 양식 및 생산
6. 우편 및 통신 서비스업
7. 항공 운송 및 철도 운송 서비스업
8. 은행 및 보험 서비스업
9. 방송 및 TV 서비스업
10. 금속 탐사, 채굴 및 수출
11. 다른 법에 따라 민간 및 전력발전 협동조합에 허가된 것 외의 전력 발전

12. 정부가 시행령/고시를 통해 지정한 안보 및 방위관련 제품의 생산

그러나 동법 규정(제II.2조)상, 상기 금지영역에 대해서도 정부는 국가의 이익을 위해 필요한 경우, 고시를 통해, 정부와 민간인 또는 다른 (민간)경제단체와의 합작이나, (미특정) 조건부로 민간인 또는 (민간)경제단체가 사업을 영위할 수 있도록 허여할 수 있도록 하고 있다.

B. 외국인 투자 금지 또는 제한 사업영역

외국인 투자법[Foreign Investment Law(FIL) of 2012] 제4조는 외국인의 투자 및 사업참여가 금지, 제한되는 사업영역에 대해 아래 (가)와 같이 일반적으로 기술(11항목)하고 있으며,

외국인 투자법에 따른 기본 시행령인 국가기획경제개발부 시행령(MNPED Notification 11/2013)에서 내국인만이 투자 가능한 25개 업종을 지정하고[아래 (나) 참조],

구체적인 투자 제한 및 승인 조건 등 상세 내역에 대해서는 외국인 투자위원회 시행령 고시를 통해 지속적으로 수정, 발표하고 있는바, 최근 고시(MIC notification No. 26/2016)에 따른 제한 및 조건부 승인 영역 및 내용은 아래 (다)와 같다.

가. 외국인투자법상 투자 금지 또는 제한 영역(11 항목)

1. 소수민족의 문화, 풍습 등을 해치는 사업

2. 국민건강에 해로운 사업

3. 자원, 자연환경 등에 해로운 사업

4. 국가에 위해하거나 유독한 폐기물 발생 우려 사업

5. 국제적으로 규정된 위험한 화학제품을 생산하는 사업
6. 해외에서 검사(미완성) 중 또는 사용허가가 발급되지 않은 기술, 의약품, 장비 등을 도입하는 사업
7. 법규, 지침으로 내국인에게만 허용된 제조업 및 서비스업 (참조: 시행령 표1)
8. 법규, 지침으로 내국인에게만 허용된 농업영역 및 장, 단기 농작물 생산 영역 (참조: 시행령 표 2)
9. 법규, 지침으로 내국인에게만 허용된 축산업 영역 (참조: 시행령 표 3)
10. 법규, 지침으로 내국인에게만 허용된 해양 어업 영역 (참조: 시행령 표4)
11. 정부허가로 지정된 경제특구 이외, 국경에서 10마일 이내 지역에서 운영하는 외국인 투자 사업

나. 외국인 투자법 시행령(MNPED Notification 11/2013)상 제한 영역

동 시행령은 외국인 투자법상 금지/제한 영역 중 상기 7~10호에 대해 아래와 같이 구체적으로 지정하고 있으며, 국가기획경제개발부(MNPED)는 동 항목들에 대해 연방정부 승인을 받아 수시로 개정할 수 있도록 규정하고 있다.

표(1): 내국인만이 할 수 있는 제조업 및 서비스업

[제조업]
1. 천연삼림 보존관리 사업
2. 전통의약품 생산사업
3. 1,000feet 이내의, 얕고 수동으로 운영되는 유정에서의 석유 생산업
4. 중소규모의 광물생산업
5. 전통약재 재배 및 생산업
6. 반가공 생산품 및 폐고철 도매업
7. 전통 음식물 제조업
8. 종교와 관련된 물품 및 용품 제조업
9. 전통적, 문화적 물품 및 용품의 제조업
10. 수공기술을 기본으로 한 상품제조업

[서비스업]
1. 전통의학 전문 개인병원
2. 전통의학 재료 관련 영업
3. 전통의학 연구 및 실험
4. 구급서비스

5. 노인건강센터 설립
6. 식당차 서비스, 상품화차 서비스, 열차청소 서비스, 열차관리 서비스
7. 중개업
8. 10MW이하의 전력생산
9. 미얀마어를 포함한 토착언어로 발행되는 정기간행물의 인쇄 및 유통

표(2): 내국인만이 할 수 있는 농업, 장/단기 농업

1. 영세(소액투자) 농업
2. 제분 및 세정 관련, 현대식 기계를 활용하지 않는 전통농업

표(3): 내국인만이 할 수 있는 축산업

1. 영세(소액투자) 축산업
2. 최신 기술을 사용하지 않는 전통방식 축산업

표(4): 내국인만이 할 수 있는 미얀마 연안 어업

1. 미얀마 대륙붕에서의 해수어, 새우 및 기타 해산물 관련 원거리 어업(far distance fishing)
2. 연못, 호수 및 기타 근거리 어업(close distance fishing)

다. 투자위원회 시행령(MIC Notification No. 26/2016)상 금지, 제한 영역

(1) 외국인에게 금지되는 업종

연번	업 종
1	국가 방위에 관련된 무기의 생산 또는 유통업
2	숲, 종교적으로 보존되어 있는 곳, 또는 종교적인 행사를 치르는 곳, 목초지, 논밭, 과수원, 수자원에 해로운 사업
3	천연 숲 관리, 보존 사업
4	옥/ 보석 탐사, 채굴 사업
5	중소규모의 광물 개발 사업
6	전력망 관리업
7	전력망 및 장비의 검사

8	항공 관제 서비스
9	강 및 연안에서의 금 또는 기타 광물자원 채취, 개발
10	해안 관제 서비스
11	인쇄(Print Media) 및 방송 미디어(Broadcasting Media) 합작사업[연방정부(Cabinet) 승인사항]
12	미얀마어 포함한 기타 소수민족 언어로 발간되는 정기간행물 유통

(2) 내국인과 합작형태로 승인되는 업종(별첨: MIC 시행령 26/2016 참조)

연번	업 종
1	과자, 와플, 국수, 쌀국수, 면 등 곡식을 이용한 생산 및 상업적 유통
2	사탕, 야자(Co Co), 초콜릿 등 간식류의 생산 및 상업적 유통
3	우유 및 유제품을 제외한 식품의 조리, 캔포장 및 상업적 유통
4	발아보리를 이용한 주류 생산 및 유통업
5	술, 소독액 등 주류 및 주류가 아닌 제품의 생산, 혼합, 정제, 포장 및 상업적 유통
6	다양한 형태의 얼음 생산 및 상업적 유통
7	정수업 및 생수업
8	다양한 종류의 원사 생산 및 상업적 유통
9	도자기, 그릇, 접시, 수저, 포크, 칼 등 다양한 형태의 주방용품의 생산 및 상업적 유통
10	다양한 형태의 플라스틱 제품의 생산 및 상업적 유통
11	포장업
12	인조 가죽 외에 신발, 핸드백, 원가죽 등을 포함한 가죽제품 생산 및 상업적 유통
13	파라핀지, 양피지, 화장실용 휴지 등 제지 및 카드보드지로부터 생산된 제지 제품의 생산 및 상업적 유통
14	국내의 천연자원을 이용한 화학제품의 생산 및 유통(석유, 천연 가스 및 관련 제품 외에)
15	불 붙기 쉬운 Acetylene, Gasoline, Propane, Hair Sprays, Perfume, Deodorant, Insect Spray 제품의 생산 및 유통

	(석유, 천연 가스 및 관련 제품 제외)
16	화학제품인(Oxygen, Hydrogen, Peroxide), 압축 가스(Acetone, Argon, Hydrogen, Nitrogen, Acetylene)의 생산 및 유통
17	화학제품인 Sulfuric Acid, Nitric Acid 의 생산 및 유통
18	산업용 화학 가스(액체, 기체, 고체)의 생산 및 유통
19	제약 원료의 생산
20	중소규모 전력 생산 사업
21	국제 수준의 골프, 리조트 개발 사업
22	아파트, 공공건물의 개발, 판매 및 임대
23	상업용 빌딩 및 사무실의 개발 및 판매
24	산업공단과 연계된 주거단지 내의 주택 건물의 개발, 판매 및 임대
25	일반 시민을 대상으로 저가형 대중주택의 개발 및 건설 사업
26	국내 여객 · 화물 항공운송 서비스
27	국제 여객 · 화물 항공운송 서비스

(3) 관련부처의 특정조건부 승인 업종(별첨: MIC 시행령 26/2016 참조)

(a) 관련 부처의 특정 조건에 의해 승인되는 업종

번호	업 종
1	농축수산부 및 지역 개발부 승인조건부 허가 업종
1	꿀벌 및 관련 벌제품 사업
2	어망 생산 공장 사업
3	물고기 부두 및 경매 가격 개발 사업
4	농축 수산물 과학 수사 연구 사업
5	바닷물고기 양어업
6	어업 제품 조리 및 생산 사업

	7	동물과 다양한 물고기 생식세포 수입/ 수출 및 목축업
	8	민물 / 바닷물고기 양어장 사업
2		환경보호 및 임업부의 승인조건부 허가 업종
	1	국립공원
	2	탄소 절감 관련 상업적 유통
	3	임업 지역(산림 경계 내/외 보호 숲)의 목재 벌채업
	4	유전자 수정 조직(Genetically Modified Organism)과 수정된 생물조직(Living Modified Organism) 등 수입 또는 생식 및 상업적 유통업
	5	귀한 목재 종자를 생산, 보호, 티슈(tissue) 키우고 생산한 임업분야 고기술 연구소 및 상업적으로 할 수 있는 사업
	6	임업분야 고기술 및 연구 개발 및 인력 개발업
	7	임업 지역 및 연방정부가 관리하는 산림지 내의 천연 자원 개발업
	8	해외로부터 또는 해외로의 나무 및 동물종자를 수입, 수출, 개발업
3		산업부의 승인조건부 허가 업종
	1	주류, 음료 및 기타 음료를 생산한 유통업
	2	조미료 생산업
	3	화학성분 합성 의약품 개발 사업
4		교통부의 승인조건부 허가 업종
	1	해양 승객 및 화물 운송 서비스 사업
	2	해양 훈련원 개발 사업
	3	조선소 사업
	4	국내 해양 운송 및 서비스 사업
5		우편통신부의 승인조건부 허가 업종
	1	국내 / 외 우송 영업
6		보건부의 승인조건부 허가 업종
	1	민간 업체가 운영하는 병원 사업
	2	민간 업체가 운영하는 진료소
	3	민간 업체가 운영하는 진찰(진단)실
	4	민간 업체가 운영하는 의약품 및 의료기기 생산업
	5	예방약 및 테스트약품 생산 연구 사업

	6	민간 업체가 운영하는 의과 대학 및 학원 사업
	7	전통 의약품 매매 사업
	8	전통 허브 재배 및 생산업
	9	전통 의약품 연구와 실험 개발 사업
	10	전통 의약품 생산 사업
	11	전통 병원 사업
7		공보부의 승인조건부 허가 업종
	1	외국어로 출판되는 신문 사업
	2	FM 라디오 방송 사업
	3	Direct To Home(DTH) 사업
	4	DVB-T 2 사업
	5	Cable TV 사업
	6	영화 제작 사업
	7	촬영 방송 사업

(b) 관련부처의 특정 조건 하에 합작으로만 승인이 허가되는 업종

	업 종	제한 요건
1	석유, 천연 가스 및 관련 재료 수입, 수출, 운송, 저장, 유통, 판매 및 이와 관련된 시설, 기계, 파이프라인 등 건설/개발 사업	에너지부와 합작으로 가능.
2	석유 및 천연 가스 탐사/채굴 및 이와 관련된 기계, 부품 등의 수입, 생산, 설치 및 개발 사업	에너지부와 합작으로 가능.
3	석유 및 천연 가스 채굴/생산 관련 실험 및 이와 관련된 기계, 부품 등 수입, 생산, 설치 및 개발 사업	에너지부와 합작으로 가능.
4	석유 및 천연 가스 운송, 파이프 라인 시스템 건축 및 이와 관련된 기계, 부품 등 수입, 생산, 설치 및 개발 사업	에너지부와 합작으로 가능.
5	다양한 해양 플랫폼 건축, 설치 및 관련 기계, 공작 기계, 부품 등 수입, 생산 및 설치 개	에너지부와 합작으로 가능.

	발 사업	
6	다양한 석유 화학공장 신설/개발, 노후 공장 재 개발 및 유통업	에너지부와 합작으로 가능.
7	담배 생산업	초기 3년간, 국산 담배잎 50%이상 사용의무, 또는 국산 담배잎의 해외 판매 수입금의 50% 한도 내 수입원료 사용 제한. 국내 생산물량의 90% 해외 수출의무. 투자 제안서에는 국내 원부자재 이용 하여야 함.
8	폭발성 물질(TNT, Nitroglycerin, Ammonium Nitrite) 생산 또는 유통업	국가와 협력, 합작형태로 가능.
9	자동적으로 불이 붙기 쉬운 기체, 고체 (Titanium Powder), Potassium Sulfide, Calcium Phosphide 생산, 유통업	국가와 협력, 합작형태로 가능.
10	곡물 수입 재배/경작 및 국내 시장에 판매 및 수출, 개발 사업	부가가치(Value-added) 제품 생산 용도 한정. 외국인 지분 최대 49% 한도. 쌀수출의 경우 해양 또는 국경 통한 무역 금지.
11	E-Lottery(E-복권) 사업	재무부 승인 필요. 정부와 합작으로만 가능.
12	신도시 개발 사업	건설부 승인 필요. 정부와 합작으로만 가능.
13	수도권 재개발 사업	건설부 승인 필요. 정부와 합작으로만 가능.
14	새로운 철로/기차역/빌딩 건축 개발 사업	미얀마 철도교통부와 합작/BOT 시스템으로 가능. 철도교통부 의견 및 내각(Cabinet) 승인 필요.
15	기차 운송 또는 수정 및 유지 사업	미얀마 철도교통부와 합작/BOT 시스템으로 가능. 철도교통부 승인 필요.
16	기차 및 화물 또는 기계 부품 설치 및 수정 개발 사업	미얀마 철도교통부와 합작/BOT 시스템으로 가능. 철도교통부 승인 필요.
17	철도교통부 소유 지역에 광케이블(Fiber Optic Cable) 연결, 타워 케이블 설치 및 기계실 건축 개발 사업	관계 사업 부처와 합작/ BOT 및 임대 시스템으로 가능. 철도교통부 승인 필요.
18	철도교통부 소유 지역 내 토지/빌딩 사용	관계 부처와 합작/ BOT 및 임대 가능. 철도교

		통부 승인 필요.
19	기차 / 차량 이용한 화물 및 승객 운송 사업	관계부처와 합작 시스템으로 가능. 철도 교통부의 의견 및 내각(Cabinet) 승인필요.
20	차량 정비 사업, 차량 운전 교육, 기계 수리 교육 및 정비 개발 사업	외국인 지분 50% 이내 합작 가능. 철도교통부 의견 필요
21	기차 사업에 사용한 전력 생산 사업	미얀마 교통부와 합작 / BOT / 임대 시스템으로 가능. 전력부 의견 및 철도교통부 승인 필요.
22	예방 의약품 생산 및 유통업	정부와의 합작사업만 가능. WHO GMP 준수하여 추진 의무.

또한,

• MIC 시행령 26/2016에 따르면, 상기 (1)~(3)에 열거된 업종외의 사업에 대해 100% 외국인 투자를 하고자 하는 경우에는 관련 부처의 승인을 득하도록 하고 있고,

• 투자와 관계없는 서비스 업종(Services not related to investment)에 대해서는 관련 부처의 승인을 득하도록 규정하고 있는바,

미얀마 원문 규정의 의미가 모호하고 광범위한 관계로, 관련 공무원들을 통해 문의해 본 결과, DICA 실무 담당관에 따라 해석상 상당한 차이를 보이고 있으므로, 상기 표상의 리스트에 해당하지 않거나, 서비스 관련 업종에 투자하고자 하는 외국인 투자자는 사전에 DICA 및 주무부서와의 협의를 통해 요건을 재확인후 진행하는 것이 바람직하다.

환경평가(Environment assessment)를 필요로 하는 사업영역을 특정하였던 MIC 시행령 No. 50/2014는, 2016년 고시된 MIC 시행령 No. 80/2016에 따라 폐지되고, 환경평가 등 관련 요건은 MIC 투자허가 심사시 관련 부처 의견 회람단계에서 해당 건별로 환경부 의견 형식을 통해 검토 및 요구되는 것으로 변경되어, 오히려 주무부서인 환경부의 법령 및 정책에 따라 탄력적으로 운영할 수 있게 되었다. 환경보호 강화 정책을 반영한 개정으로 해석된다.

Ⅳ. 외국인 투자 인센티브

항 목	외국인 투자법(FIL)	특별경제구역법(SEZL)		
		면세지구 (exempted zone) 또는 면세업 투자	진흥지구 (promotion zone) 또는 기타 사업 투자	개발업자
소득세 면세 Income Tax Exemption	최초 5년간, 이후 MIC 재량으로 감면(면제 또 는 경감) 연장가능	최초 7년간	최초 5년간	최초 8년간
소득세 경감 Income Tax Relief	이익 유보금을 1년 이 내 재투자한 경우, 해 당 이익에 대한 소득세 감면	최초 면세기간 후(두 번째), 5년간 소득세 50% 경감		
	수출 상품에 대한 이익 의 50%까지 소득세 경감	이후(세번째) 5년간, 이익유보금을 1년 이내에 재투자하는 경우, 해당 이익에 대한 소득세 경감		
관세 감면 Custom Duty	건설기간 동안, 사용하 기 위해 수입한 기계, 장비, 부품, 기타 자재 등에 대한 관세 및 기 타 세금 감면	면세 지구에서 생 산 또는 건설 위해 수입한 원자재, 기 계, 장비, 차량 및 기타 제품 등에 대 한 관세 및 기타 세 금 면제	- 최초 5년 동안, 건 설 위해 수입한 기계 및 장비에 대한 관세 및 기타 세금 면제 - 이후 5년간은, 50% 경감	건설 위해 수입한 원자재, 차량, 기 계, 장비 및 기타 상품에 대한 관세 및 기타 세금 면제
	건설 완료 후 상업 생 산의 첫 3년 동안 수입 한 원자재에 대한 관세 and/or 기타 내국세 감 면	도매유통, 수출 및 물류에 필요한 자 동차 및 기타 제품 수입시 관세, 기타 세금 면제	수입된 원재료 및 다 른 제품을 이용하여 만든 완성품 또는 반 제품을 수출 또는 면 세지역으로 반입시 관세 환급 가능	
	MIC 승인을 받아, 투			

	자 증가 및 당초 사업 확장한 경우, 확장 사업상 필요로 수입한 기계, 장비, 도구, 부품, 예비부품 및 재료 등에 대한 관세 and/or 내국세 감면			
상업세 Commercial Tax	수출용으로 제조된 상품에 대한 상업세 감면	* 수출용 상품/서비스에 대해서는 면세 * 면제지구 투자자: 원칙적으로 면세적용, 내국 또는 진흥지구로부터 수입한 제품에 대해서도 상업세 면제 * 진흥지구 투자자는 별도 시행령이 정한 감면기간 동안 상업세 감면 가능 * 상기 관세감면 항목에 대해서는 상업세도 감면
공제 Deduction	MIC가 허여한 비율에 따라 기계, 장비, 건물 및 기타 자본재에 대해 조기 감가상각하고, 이를 소득 공제대상 비용으로 처리가능			
	R&D 비용을 소득에서 공제 처리 가능	* 훈련비 및 R&D 비용, 소득공제 가능
	소득세 면세기간(tax holiday) 후 연속된 2년 기간이내에 발생한 순손실을 발생연도로부터 3년까지 순손실 공제 이월 처리 가능	* 순손실 발생연도로부터 5년간 이월 공제가능
내국인 세율 적용	외국인 종업원에게 지불한 임금에 대해 미얀마 시민과 동일한 소득세율 적용 가능	* Union Tax Law 개정으로, 2015.4.1일 이후 소득에 대해, 내/외국인 구별없이 모두 동일세율 적용
토지 이용권	최초 50년간 임대가능하고, 이후 10년씩 2회 연장가능(총 70년 임대가능)	최초 50년까지 임대 가능하고, 이후 25년간 연장 가능(총 75년 임대가능)

* Tax holiday(최초 5년간 소득세 면제) 외의 인센티브는 MIC 투자 허가시 자동으로 허여되는 것이 아니므로, 외국인투자법 기본시행령(MNPED Notification 11/2013)에 따라 MIC Form 10상에 인센티브 받고자 하는 항목을 명기하여, MIC에 그러한 허여를 구체적으로 요청하여야 함을 유의 바람.

[참고] **상업세 및 관세 감면혜택 배제 사업영역**

MIC 시행령 No. 51/2014에 따라, 외국인투자법 및 미얀마 시민투자법상 허여될 수 있는 상업세 및 관세 감면혜택은 아래 사업영역에서는 적용이 배제된다.

2014.8.19 이후 MIC 투자허가 사업에 대해 발효. 발효일 이전에 이미 투자허가된 사업에 허여된 감면혜택은 지속됨.

상업세 및 관세 감면혜택 배제 사업

---

a. 주류, 맥주, 담배류 및 유사 제품과 관련 서비스업

b. 가솔린, 디젤유, 엔진오일 및 천연가스 판매, 유통

c. 차량 정비/유지 및 유사 서비스

d. 고도기술이나 최소자본 투자 없이 미얀마 시민이 영위할 수 있는 산업(노동집약사업 제외)

e. 숲(보존/보호림 지역)에 대한 장기임대 통한 생산, 채취(벌목)

f. 천연자원 채취(원유 및 가스 채취 및 생산 제외)

g. 건물 건축 및 판매

h. 자동차, 기계 및 장비 임대업

i. 식당 및 식음료 사업

상업세 감면혜택 배제 사업(관세 혜택은 허용)

낙농(milk & dairy) 관련 식품업

V. 조세 개요(2016년 4월 1일 기준)

• **관련 법규:**

개정 소득세법(Amended Income Tax Law of 1974: ITL)

개정 상업세법(Amended Commercial Tax Law of 1990: CTL)

2014년 연방세법, 2015년 연방세법, 2016년 연방세법(Union Tax Law of 2016)

• **세무/회계연도**

매년 4/1~다음해 3/31

• **거주자 기준:**

i) 미얀마에 주소지(domicile)를 둔 사람,

ii) 해당 과세연도 중 최소 183일 이상 미얀마 거주 외국인,

iii) FIL 회사에 근무 중인 외국인(거주기간 무관). (단, 미얀마 원천 소득에만 과세)

• **과세대상 소득 범위**

거주자: 미얀마 국내 소득은 물론 해외발생 소득도 미얀마 소득세 과세

비거주자: 미얀마 국내 원천 소득에 대해서만 과세

FIL 회사는 거주자로 간주되지만, 해외 원천 소득에 대해서는 비과세.

• 영미법상 조합과는 달리, 미얀마법상 조합은 직접 과세대상임(조합의 소득이 각 투자자의 투자 지분 등의 비율로 투자자에게 이전 과세되지 않음).

• 미얀마와 이중과세방지 협약국:

인도, 라오스, 말레이지아, 싱가폴, <u>대한민국</u>, 태국, 영국, 베트남

* 한국-미얀마 조세협약상 제한세율: 이자 10%, 배당 10%, 특허 등 지적재산권 및 기술 사용료 10%, 기타 사용료 15%

분류	납세자	세율	비고
법인세[1][2]	회사법에 따라 설립된 법인	25%	2015.4.1.부터 동일세율 적용
	외국인투자법에 따라 설립된 법인		
	특별허가를 통해 미얀마정부 프로젝트("SS 프로젝트")에 참여중인 외국 기관/단체		
	외국기업의 지점[3] (FIL 투자허가 법인 여부 무관)		
	협동조합(Cooperative Societies)		2016.4.1.부터 동일세율 적용
	국유 경제기관		
개인소득세 (급여,[4] 전문소득 및 기타 혜택)	소득액 4,800,000 Ks 이하	0%(면세)	2016.4. 회계연도 소득분부터 적용
	시민 및 외국국적 거주자	0%: ~ 2MKs 5%: ~ 5MKs 10%: ~ 10MKs 15%: ~ 20MKs 20%: ~ 30MKs 25%: over 30MKs	누진세율. 2015.4.1.부터 동일 세율 적용
	FIL 법인에서 근무하는 외국인 (거주자로 간주)		
	FIL 법인이 아닌 기타 법인에서 일하는 비거주자		
재산세	토지 임대, 건물 및 아파트 임대료 소득 * 다른 소득과 결합 또는 추가 과세 않음.	10%	
해외소득	해외거주 시민의 해외 원천 소득 총액 * 공제 적용 안 됨.	10%	
탈루(미신고)소득	(1) 모든 미신고(탈루) 소득에 일괄 적용 (공제 적용 허용 안 됨) (2) 신규 또는 확장 사업 구매, 건설, 매입 또는 설립용도로	30%	

	사용된 경우, 소득원이 증명된 금액 공제후 잔여(미증명) 금액에 한해, 아래 기준에 따라 차등 과세:		
	1~ 30,000,000 Ks	15%	
	~100,000,000 Ks	20%	
	100,000,000 Ks 초과	30%	
사회보장기금	종업원 고용주	급여의 2% 급여의 3%	월간 6,000 Ks 한도 월간 9,000 Ks 한도
공제	a. 기본공제 Basic Relief b. 부양(동거) 부모공제 c. 배우자 공제 d. 생활 보험료 공제 e. 자녀 공제 f. 사회보장기금 공제	a. 소득의 20% b. 1MKs/명 c. 1MKs d. 실제 비용 e. 0.5M/명 f. 실제 비용	a. 최대 10MKs d. 배우자보험료 포함 e. 18세미만 또는 학생
손금이월	납세자는 3년까지 손금 이월 가능(사단법인의 손금, 손금지 분은 제외)		
양도소득세[5]	거주자 및 비거주자 개인 및 법인 * 양도소득 5,000,000Ks 이하 면세	10%	2015.4.1.부터 동일률 적용
이익배당세	거주자 및 비거주자 동일 적용 * 원천소득에 대해 1단계 과세	0%	법인소득세 과세 후, 배당에 대해서는 추가 과세 않음
원천징수세	거주자 a. 이자 b. Royalties c. 정부 지불료[6] d. 미등록 외국법인지불료[7]	a. 0% b. 15% c. 2% d. 2%	
	비거주자 (a) (b) (c) (d)	a. 15% b. 20% c. 3.5% d. 3.5%	
간접세 및 기타 세금			
상업세 Commercial Tax[8]	a. 국내 생산/판매된 제품 또는 제공된 서비스에 대해서는 판매가 또는 서비스료에 상업	5%	제외: (a) Special Goods (List A 참조)

	세 부과 b. 수입제품에 대해서는 국내 도착가격(CIF 가격 및 관세포함)을 기초로 관세청에서 상업세 부과	5%	(b) 면세 상품 (List B 참조) (c) 면제세비스 (List C 참조)
	입국항공운송 서비스	3%	
	개발업자의(건축후) 건물판매 수익	3%	
	* 해당 회계연도 중 상업세부과 대상 제품/용역 수입총액이 20,000,000Ks 미만인 경우, 면제.		
	수출 상품: 단, 아래품목은 상업세 부과: a. 원유 b. 천연가스 c. 티크 및 단단한 원목 d. 옥, 보석 및 귀금속 e. (d)로 만든 장신구 f. 전력	0% 5% 8% 50% 15% 5% 8%	
인지세 Stamp duty	각종 법정 서류 및 일반용도의 비법정 서류에 부과 • 부동산 판매/양도: 가액의 3% + 추가 2% (양곤소재 부동산) • 주식판매 및 양도: 0.3% • 채권판매 및 양도: 2% • 부동산 임대(1년~3년): 1.5% (연간 임대료 기준) • 부동산 임대 (3년 초과): 3% (연간임대료 + 프리미엄)		- Stamp Act of 1891 - 개정안, 2014.4. 발효
관세 Custom Duty	대부분 수입제품은 수입시 관세 대상이며, 관세청 신고 의무. 일반적인 관세율 0% ~ 40% * FIL 및 SEZL에 따른 외국인 투자에 대한 감면혜택 가능 * 일반적으로, 보세장치구역 경유 후 재수출시 기납부된 관세액의 7/8 환급 가능(Sea Customs Act of 1878)		미얀마 관세법, 2012
재산세 Property Tax[9]	과세자: 지방도시개발위원회 납세자: 부동산(토지 및 건물) 소유자 양곤시 소재 재산 기준: a. 종합세(general tax) b. 조명세(lighting tax) c. 용수세(water tax) d. 관리세(conservancy tax)	 8% 이하 5% 이하 6.5% 이하 3.25% 이하	해당 토지/건물의 (예상) 임대료 총액을 과표로 세율 적용. * 가구 및 집기 제공 조건 임대 기준

1 사업개시연도 포함 초기 3년간 10,000,000Ks 이내 소득규모의 중소기업은 법인소득세 면제되고, 그 금액을 초과한 금액에 대해서만 법인소득세가 부과됨.

2 석유 및 천연가스 업종 기업에 대해서는 다음과 같은 별도 소득세율 적용.

1,000 억 Ks 이하	40%
~1,500 억 Ks	45%
1,500 억 Ks 초과	50%

3 일반적으로 외국 기업의 지점은 비거주자(회사)로 간주.

4 임금(근로수입)은 임시 지급 수당 및 각종 혜택을 포함하며, 고용주가 종업원의 개인소득세를 대납한 경우에는 대납세금을 포함한 합산액(tax on tax)을 기초로 소득세를 산정함.

5 석유 및 가스 회사의 주식에 대한 양도소득세는 다음과 같은 별도 세율이 적용됨(거주자 및 비거주자 동일 세율).

Up to 100 billion Ks	40%
~ 150 billion Ks	45%
Over 150 billion Ks	50%

6 연방정부, 지방정부 및 기타 관련 법규에 따라 설립된 공적 기관, 기구, 단체 등("정부기관")에게 제공된 상품 및 용역에 대한 대가로 지불된 금액(지불자: 정부기관).

7 미얀마에서 등록되지 않은 외국 법인에게 미얀마 내국에서 제공된 구매 및 서비스에 대한 대가로 지불된 금액(지불자: 미등록 외국법인).

8 상업세는 미얀마에서의 부가가치세가 아니라 상품과 용역에 대한 거래세 성격으로 부과된다.

9 외국인(기업)은 미얀마에서 부동산을 소유할 수 없기 때문에 (부동산) 재산세는 외국인에게는 적용되지 않는다.

[참고] 특별 상업세 부과 항목 및 상업세 면세항목

* 2016년 Union Tax Law 기준

[LIST A: 특별상업세 부과 항목]

· 술, 담배, 고급 차량 및 보석, 티크, 천연가스, 석유등에 대해서, 아래 표와 같이 5~120%의 특별 상업세 부과

No	특별품목	시장가 기준 가치	세 율
1	Cigarettes (20개비 1팩 기준)	300Ks이하	3Ks/개비
		301Ks ~ 500Ks	8Ks/개비
		501Ks ~ 1,000Ks	14Ks/개비
		1,001Ks ~ 2,000Ks	29Ks/개비
		2,001Ks ~ 3,000 Ks	48Ks/개비
		3,000Ks 초과	시장가의 120%
	Cigarettes(수입)	국내 통관 가격	120%
2	Tobacco		60%
3	Virginia tobacco, cured		60%
4	Cheroot		60%
5	Cigars		60%
6	Pipe tobacco		60%
7	Betel chewing preparation		60%
8	주류 (1리터 기준)	500Ks / 리터	66Ks/리터
		501Ks ~ 1,000Ks	197Ks
		1,001Ks ~ 2,000Ks	394Ks
		2,001Ks ~ 3,000Ks	656Ks
		3,001Ks ~ 4,000Ks	919Ks

		4,001Ks ~ 5,000Ks	1,181Ks
		5,001Ks ~ 7,000Ks	1,575Ks
		7,001Ks ~ 10,000Ks	2,231Ks
		10,000Ks 초과	시장가의 60%
	주류(수입)	국내통관가격	통관가의 60%
9	맥주		60%
10	와인		50%
11	티크, 원목 및 가공품		25%
12	보석류(Jade, rubies, sapphires, emeralds, diamonds 등)		15%
13	보석가공품		5%
14	1800 CC이상 픽업차량, 밴, 경승합차, 사롱, 세단, 웨곤 및 쿠페 등 고급 차량		25%
15	휘발유, 디젤유, 항공제트 연료		10%
16	천연가스		8%

50

[LIST B: 상업세 면세 상품]

- 상업세 면세항목은, 주로 아래 유형의 물품을 포함 (1~73호)

  - 식량, 식품, 의약품, 교재 및 학용품, 종교용품 등 생활필수품
  - 국가 안보(국방, 치안 및 소방/구급 등) 관련 물자, 장비 및 차량

- 예외적으로, 아래와 같은 특정 유형의 구매자(외교, 원조, 면세점 판매, 출국 항공 관련자 등)에게 판매되는 항목을 포함하고 있다. (74~81호)

  - 출국시 외국인 승객에게 외화판매되는 면세용품
  - 외교관, 대사관 및 영사관 직원 사용용도 물품(상호주의 조건)
  - 국방부 예산으로 구매하여 군대에 배급될 물품
  - OEM등 위탁생산 제품용 원부자재, 포장용기
  - 외국대사관, UN기구 및 외교관에게 동력부(Ministry of Energy)가 판매한 연료에너지
  - 현지 및 외국 기관이 국가 원조기금으로 구매한 물품
  - 출국 항공기용 연료
  - 정부의 필요에 따라 의회가 면세를 인정한 상품

no.	품 목
1.	벼, 쌀, 피, 겨, 껍질(Paddy, rice, split, soft bran, rough bran, paddy husk)
2.	밀, 밀가루(Wheat grain, flour, smooth and rough flour)
3.	옥수수, 옥수수 가루, 기타 곡물 및 곡물 가루(Maize and other cereals, powder maize and other powder cereals)
4.	말린 씨앗, 완두콩, 콩가루(Pulses, chick peas, pea flour)
5.	땅콩(Peanuts, shelled or unshelled)
6.	참깨(Sesame, sesame flowers)
7.	겨자씨, 해바라기씨, 타마린드, 목화씨(Mustard seeds, sunflower seeds, tamarind seeds, cotton seeds)
8.	야자오일 (Palm oil)
9.	각종 목화 (Various cottons)

10.	황마 및 유사 섬유질(Jute and similar fibers)
11.	마늘, 양파(Garlic, onions)
12.	감자(Potatoes)
13.	카사바 및 카사바 가루(Cassava plants, cassava powder)
14.	향신료 및 가공 양념[Spices(leaves, fruits, seeds, bark), prepared spices]
15.	각종 과일(Various fresh fruits)
16.	야채(Vegetables)
17.	설탕, 사탕수수(Sugar, sugarcane)
18.	뽕나무 잎(Mulberry leaves)
19.	약초 및 허브(Medical plants or herbs)
20.	야자가지, 갈대, 기타 농작물(Thatch, reeds, thapo, dani, taung htan, pharlar, elephant foot yam tuber, thanakhar and such agricultural products not elsewhere specified)
21.	나무, 대나무(Wood, bamboo)
22.	동물, 물고기, 새우(Live animals, fish and shrimps)
23.	누에고치(Silk cocoons)
24.	설탕수수(Canes, finished and unfinished)
25.	벌꿀 및 밀랍(Honey and bee wax)
26.	천연염료 랙(Lac)
27.	땅콩, 깨, 겨, 콩 등 기름짠 후 찌꺼기(Dregs from the production of peanut oil, sesame oil, bran oil, fermented soy-bean oil and solid oil)
28.	가루비누, 비누(Soap powder, soap)
29.	표백유(Bleaching oil)
30.	코코넛 껍질로 만든 실 및 숯(Coir yarn, charcoal made from coconut shells)
31.	차잎 및 말린 녹차류(Tea leaves, various kinds of dry tea leaves)
32.	각종 우표 및 인지(Different kinds of stamps, including revenue stamps)
33.	봉랍 및 인장(Sealing wax and sticks)
34.	슬레이트, 슬레이트 연필 및 분필(Slates, slate pencils and chalk)
35.	새우 및 생선 소스[Shrimp and fish sauces(ngan-pya-ya)]
36.	땅콩오일, 참기름, 해바라기유, 겨기름, 간장, 된장(Peanut oil, sesame oil, sunflower oil, bran oil, fermented soy-bean oil, solid oil)
37.	생선, 생새우(Raw fish, raw prawns)
38.	우유 및 우유가루 제품 (Milk, all kinds of milk powder)
39.	고추, 고추가루(Chili, chili powder)
40.	사프란, 사프란 가루(Saffron, saffron powder)
41.	생강(Ginger)
42.	어묵(Fish paste)
43.	익은 타마린드(Ripe tamarinds)
44.	국기(National flag)

45.	종교용 염주(Various kinds of religious beads)
46.	각종 자, 지우개, 연필깎이(Various kinds of rulers, erasers, sharpeners)
47.	땔감 대체재료(Alternatives to firewood)
48.	코코넛오일[야자유 제외, Coconut oil (not palm oil)]
49.	각종 계란(Various kinds of fowl eggs)
50.	호박씨, 수박씨(Pumpkin seeds, watermelon seeds)
51.	승복 등 종교의상[Religious clothes (thingyan robes, etc.)]
52.	기름찌꺼기(Oil dregs)
53.	소금(Salt)
54.	고무 반죽(Rubber paste)
55.	씹는 청량제 버틀넛(Betel nuts)
56.	비료(Fertilizers)
57.	살충제(Insecticides, pesticides)
58.	농기구, 농기계 및 부품(Farm equipment, farm machines and parts)
59.	동물 사료 및 사료용 원료(Raw materials for animal feed, finished animal feed)
60.	동물 의약품(Animal medicines)
61.	교잡육종 성분(Cross-breeding components)
62.	태양광용 패널, 충전기, 컨트롤러, 인버터 등(Solar panels, solar charger controllers and solar inverters)
63.	엑스레이용 필름, 판, 재료, 및 수술, 의료, 약제 도구 및 장비(X-ray films, plates and other X-ray material, surgical, medical or pharmaceutical apparatus and equipment)
64.	반창고, 거즈, 소독제, 기타 병원 및 외과용 치료제, 약제(Bandages, gauze, other surgical dressing materials, hospital and surgical outfit and sundries)
65.	(법령상 제한 품목 제외한) 약품 및 기타 의약품[Pharmaceutical and other medicines (except medicine restricted by rules and regulations)]
66.	약품 원재료(Raw materials for pharmaceuticals)
67.	교과서, 연습장, 스케치북, 기타 서적용 종이류 및 연필류(Textbooks, exercise and drawing books of various kinds and papers for the production of such books and all sorts of pencils)
68.	연필심(Graphite for the production of pencils)
69.	콘돔(Condoms)
70.	국방/안보 용도로 정부기관이 사용하는 무기, 기계, 차량, 장비 및 부품(weapons, machines, vehicles, equipment and their spare parts for the usage of governmental organizations for national defense and security)
71.	정부부서용 화약, 다이너마이트 및 부속품류(Various kinds of gun powder, various kinds of dynamites and accessories thereof used by the civil departments)
72.	농작물 씨앗, 육종용 식물(Crops seeds, nursery plants)
73.	소방차, 구급차(Fire engines, ambulance vehicles)

74.	출국시 외국인 승객에게 외화판매되는 면세용품
75.	외교관 및 대사관/영사관 직원 사용 물품(상호주의 조건)
76.	국방부 예산으로 구매하여 군대에 배급될 물품
77.	OEM등 위탁생산 제품용 원부자재, 포장용기
78.	외국대사관, UN기구 및 외교관에게 동력부(Ministry of Energy)가 판매한 연료 에너지
79.	현지 및 외국 기관이 국가 원조기금으로 구매한 물품
80.	출국 항공기용 연료
81.	정부의 필요에 따라 의회가 면세를 인정한 상품

[LIST C: 면세 서비스]

- 주로 대중 편의 시설 및 공중 업무관련 서비스가 면세항목에 해당되며(1~23호),
- 예외적으로 국방부, 국가행정기관 및 외교/원조 관련 단체에 제공된 서비스도 포함되어 있음(24~29호).

No.	서비스 유형
1	상업적이 아닌 주택 임대업
2	주차장 임대업
3	생명보험업
4	소규모 금융업(Microfinance)
5	건강관리업
6	교육사업
7	화물운송업(차량, 선박, 항공, 중장비 운송업 등)
8	취업알선업
9	투자시장(증권/채권 매매 등) 관련 서비스
10	은행업무
11	통관업무
12	외식 및 행사 대행업
13	OEM 등 계약 생산업
14	장례업
15	육아업
16	미얀마 전통마사지/ 맹인 안마
17	이사업
18	통행료징수업
19	동물 수의업

20	공중화장실 요금징수업
21	출국항공 운송업
22	문화예술업
23	대중교통업(버스, 철도, 여객선 등)
24	정부기관에 지불하는 라이선스료
25	국방부 안보관련 출판업
26	외교관 및 대사관/영사관 직원에 제공된 서비스(상호주의 조건)
27	현지 및 외국기관이 국가 원조기금으로 지불하는 서비스
28	정부 필요 용도로 의회에서 면세승인된 서비스
29	연방정부 부처, 대통령실, 법무장관실, 감사실, 의회, 기타 연방기구, 위원회, 중앙은행, 네피도 시정부, 지방정부 등 연방 및 지방 정부기구 상호간 제공 업무(단, 국영기업이 제공하거나 제공받은 업무는 제외)

VI. 투자보장
Investment Protection

투자보장 관련, 대부분 국가의 외국인투자법상 일반적인 관례는:

(i) 관련 세금 납부후 투자금과 과실의 본국 회수 및 송금 보장

(ii) 투자 사업 및 자산의 일방적 국유화 금지 보장

(iii) 공익 등 적법사유로 국유화할 경우, 적정 보상(시장가격 등에 기초) 보장.

또한, 일반적으로 대부분 국가의 외국인 투자법규는 외국인 투자자가 정부당국과의 투자관련 분쟁을 국제 중재를 통하여 해결할 수 있는 선택권을 제공하고 있다(아래 VIII. B. 참조).

이와 관련된 미얀마 법규를 살펴보면,

우선 연방헌법[36조 (d)항]은 기업들에 대한 국유화 금지 규정을 두고 있으며, 외국인 투자법은 외국인 투자자에 대해 아래와 같은 법적 보호 규정을 두고 있다.

A. 외화 송금(Right to transfer foreign currency)

외국인 투자자는, 아래 조건을 충족한 경우, 미얀마법규상 외환거래서비스가 허가된 은행을 통하여 송금시점의 적용환율에 따라 외화를 해외로 송금할 수 있다.

- 당초 투자시 미얀마에 외화자금으로 반입한 경우 외화로 송금을 허여함.
- 미얀마투자위원회 승인을 받아 미얀마에 반입한 자본의 인출, 회수를 허여함.
- 외국인 투자자의 연간 수익에서 관련 세금, 사회복지기금 및 기타 공과금을 공제한 순이익의 송금을 허여함.
- 외국인 근로자의 경우, 관련 세금 및 미얀마 생활비 등을 공제한 급여 및 기타 적법한 수입액의 잔여금의 송금을 허여함.

B. 보장(Guarantee)

외국인 투자법 규정에 따르면, 정부는 투자위원회가 승인한 외국인 투자에 대해, 계약기간 중 또는 (연장시) 연장기간 중 국유화 금지를 보장하고 있다.

또한, 허가기간 중 적정사유(sufficient cause) 없이 투자가 취소되지 않을 것을 보장함과 동시에 투자계약기간 만료시에는 해당 외국인 자본이 투자자들에게 이전/회수될 것을 보장하고 있다.

경제특구(Special Economic Zone)에 대한 투자에 대해서는,
미얀마 경제특구법(SEZ Law)에 따라,
- 국유화 금지를 보장하고,
- 면세구역(exempted zones) 및 장려구역(promoted zones)에서 생산된 제품이나 제공된 서비스에 대한 수출/제공 가격에 대해서는 자유책정을 보장한다(정부 통제 금지).

C. 국제투자협약상 보호

외국인 투자법 또는 기타 미얀마 법규상 보호 외에도, 미얀마와 투자보호협약(2

자간 상호 협약 또는 ASEAN 등 다자간 협약)을 맺은 국가에 설립지를 둔 외국인 투자자(기업)의 경우에는 해당 투자협약상의 규정에 따른 보호혜택을 받을 수 있다.

한국인(기업)의 경우, 한-아세안 투자협약(ASEAN-Korea Investment Agreement, 2009년 6월 2일 체결, 2009년 9월 1일 발효) 및 한-미얀마 투자보호협약(Investment Protection Agreement between Myanmar and Korea, 2014년 6월 5일 체결, 현재까지 미발효)의 적용을 받을 수 있다.

참고로, OECD는 미얀마의 투자보호 법규에 대해 아래와 같이 문언적 문제점을 지적하고 있으나, 미얀마 정부나 법원 판례에서 아래 미비 규정을 보장제한으로 해석한 사례도 없음은 물론, 일부 명문규정 미비에 따른 관련 이슈는, 미얀마가 체결한 여러 투자협약상 규정과 국제 관례 및 원칙 등을 근거로 보완적 해석이 가능한 것으로 보이므로, 외국인 투자자에게 국제적 관례나 원칙에 반한 불이익이나 문제점을 야기할 것으로 보이지는 않는다. (참조: OECD Investment Policy Reviews: Myanmar 2014; 아래에 비평 요지를 번역, 요약함)

연방헌법 및 외국인투자법은 국유화 또는 몰수를 금지하고 있으나, (i) 간접적인 몰수 금지 규정이나 (ii) 몰수시 적시, 적정(시장가격 등) 보상을 요구하는 Hull Rule과 같은 규정이 없다. 반면, 미얀마가 체결한 대부분의 양자 간 투자협약상에는 다음과 같이 간접적인 금지 규정이 존재한다.

"Investment shall not be nationalized, expropriated or subject to measures having an effect equivalent to nationalization or expropriation."

반면, 통상적인 국제 관례와는 달리, 연방협법이나 외국인 투자법, 경제특구법은 국가의 주권 보호 규정에 따른 유보 조항을 두고 있지 않다. 즉, 국제관례 및 원칙상, 각국 정부는 공익상(경제, 정치, 사회적 사유) 필요시, 공정한 기준과 적법절차 및 적정 보상 원칙에 따라 관련 자산을 국유화, 몰수할 수 있는 주권행사 유보조항을 둘 수 있으나, 미얀마 법규상으로는 이런 주권 유보 원칙에 대한 명문 조항이 존재하지 않고, 오히려 미얀마가 체결한 대부분의 국제협약상에는 이러한 원칙이 규정되어 있다.

VII. 국제경제협약
International Economic Agreements

미얀마가 현재까지 체결한 경제협력 및 투자보호 관련 양자간 또는 다자간 주요 협약 현황(한국과의 협약 외는 발효 계약 한정)은 아래와 같다.

양자간 투자 협약	필리핀	발효 (1998년)
	중국	발효 (2002년)
	인도	발효 (2009년)
	태국	발효 (2012년)
	일본	발효 (2014년)
	이스라엘, 쿠웨이트, 베트남, 라오스	*체결 / 미발효*
	한국	미발효 (2014년 체결)
이중과세방지협약	인도, 라오스, 말레이지아, 싱가폴, 태국, 영국, 베트남	발효
	한국	2003년 8월 4일 발효
벵갈만 기술/경제 협력을 위한 (다자간) 발기 협약	뱅글라데시, 부탄, 인도, 미얀마, 네팔, 스리랑카, 태국협약(the Bay of Bengal Initiative for Multi-Sector Technical and Economic Cooperation)	2017년까지 경제자유지역 형성을 목표로 체결된 기본협약
ASEAN 회원국 상호 간 협약(다자 협약)	아세안 종합투자 협약 ASEAN Comprehensive Investment Agreement(ACIA)	

	아세안 자유무역지역 협약 ASEAN Free Trade Area(AFTA)
	아세안 서비스 관련 기본 협약 ASEAN Framework Agreement on Services(AFAS)
	아세안투자지역 관련 기본 협약 Framework Agreement on ASEAN Investment Area(AIA)
ASEAN 투자협약 (ASEAN 회원국과 해당국 간의 협약) * 미얀마도 회원국으 로서 해당 체약국과 효력 발생	ASEAN-China Free Trade Agreement (2010 발효) ASEAN-Japan Agreement on Comprehensive Economic Partnership (2003 발효) ASEAN-India Framework Agreement on Comprehensive Economic Agreement (2004 발효) Agreement for ASEAN-Australia-New Zealand Free Trade Area (2012 발효)
	ASEAN-Korea Investment Agreement * 2009년 6월 2일 체결, 2009년 9월 1일 발효
	ASEAN-Korea Framework Agreement on Comprehensive Economic Cooperation * 2007년 6월 1일 발효, 2009년 1월 1일까지 90% 품목 관세철폐, 2018년까지 관세 완전철폐, 상품 자유무역지역 형성을 목표로 체결된 협약

VIII. 투자관련 분쟁 해결

A. 미얀마 법원 사법절차

미얀마의 법원 제도와 조직은 2008년 헌법 제6장과 2010년의 연방 법원조직법 (Union Judiciary Act of 2010)에 따라 구성되어 있다.

미얀마 법원은 아래와 같이 3단계로 구성되어 있다:
  ① 대법원(Supreme Court)
  ② 14개 지방 또는 자치주 상급법원(Region or State High Courts)
  ③ 자치구, 지구, 타운 법원(Courts of the self-administered divisions or zones; District Courts, Township Courts)

일반적으로 통상적인 재판은 1차로 타운 법원, 기초 행정지역 관할법원에서 진행되며, 1심 법원의 판결은 지방 또는 자치주 상급법원에 항소할 수 있고, 최종적으로 대법원에 상고할 수 있다.

대법원은 최종심 법원 기능 외에도, 최고법원으로서 모든 하급 법원에 대한 관리, 감독권을 가지며, 미얀마 정부가 체결한 국제조약/협약 등과 관련된 사안에 대한 최초(original) 관할권을 가진다.

미얀마 법제는 영국계 보통법과 성문법 체제가 혼용되어 있으나, 배심원 제도는 없으며, 재판은 일반적으로 단독 판사에 의해 진행된다. 단, 사안에 따라 대법관의 특별지시에 의해 복수의 판사로 구성된 재판부가 사건을 심리, 재판하는 경우도 있다.

상술한 일반 법원 외에도 군사법원과 헌법재판소와 같은 특별법원도 존재한다.

행정부와 군부가 여전히 재판 절차와 판사 임명 및 해임에 상당한 영향력을 행사하고 있는 관계로, 사법부의 역량 및 독립성이 미흡하여 미얀마에서 사업을 하고 있는 외국인 투자자들은 미얀마 법원을 통한 분쟁 해결보다는 국제중재를 통한 해결을 선호하고 있다.

B. 미얀마 중재법(Arbitration Law of 2016)

2016년 1월 5일, 연방의회가 새로운 중재법[Arbitration Law of 2016(Union Law 5/2016; 신 중재법)]을 통과, 발효함에 따라, 국내 중재법상 외국에서의 중재판정 선택 허용여부, 외국 중재판정의 효력 및 국내에서의 집행력 인정등과 관련한 보장이 미흡하고, 국내법원의 국내 중재 관여권이 강했던, 1944년 구 중재법(Arbitration Act of 1944)은 완전 폐지되고, 신 중재법으로 대체되어,

미얀마 의회가 2013년 7월 15일 인준, 발효한 외국중재판정의 효력 인정과 집행에 관한 뉴욕협약(the New York Convention on the Recognition and Enforcement of Foreign Arbitral Awards: "뉴욕협약")을 완전히 이행할 수 있는 내국법제도를 완비하게 되었다.

신 중재법은 국제적으로 인정, 통용되는 중재절차와 관례를 반영한 UNICITRAL 표준 중재법에 상당한 기초를 둔 입법이다. 신 중재법의 시행에 따라 구 중재법과 뉴욕협약 규정 간의 불일치 및 차이 등으로 인한 종전의 문제점은 최종적으로 해소되게 되었다.

따라서, 뉴욕협약의 제반 규정을 준수한 신 중재법하에서는 당사자는,

(i) 당사자 간의 상업적 분쟁해결을 해외에서의 중재를 통해 해결하는 선택을 자유롭게 합의할 수 있고

(ii) 이러한 합의 중재가 선택된 사건에 대해서는 어느 일방이 법원에 재판을 청구하더라도, 법원은 중재판정시까지 재판절차 진행을 보류하게 되며,

(iii) 뉴욕협약 체약국 내에서 이루어진 외국중재판정에 대해 미얀마 법원은 그 효력을 인정하고, 그에 따른 집행을 허가하게 된다.

단, 현재까지 미얀마에는 상설 중재기구가 존재하지 않으며, 실무상, 미얀마에서의 국제상사분쟁에 대한 중재는 미얀마 상공회의소(상설중재기구가 아닌 ad hoc 중재포럼 역할)를 통해 이루어지고 있다.

한편, 관련 계약 당사자들 간의 계약관련 분쟁 해결을 위해 국제상사중재를 선택할 수 있는 반면, 현재까지 미얀마는 ICSID 협약(1965 Convention on Settlement of Investment Disputes between States and Nationals of other States; 현재 143개 가입국)의 체약국이 아닌 관계로, 투자자와 국가(정부당국) 간의 분쟁 해결을 위한 ICSID 중재는 인정되고 있지 않다. 일반적으로 여타 ad hoc 중재 포럼과 비교할 때, ICSID 중재판정은 국내법원에서의 재판과 동일한 효력을 인정받는 관계로, 외국중재판정에 대한 효력인정 및 집행과 관련한 내국법의 적용을 받지 않고, 내국법원은 ISCID중재 절차에 관여할 수 없다는 장점이 있다.

IX. 노동법

A. 관련법규

미얀마의 노동관련 법규는 다른 영역의 법규들처럼, 단일 법규가 아니라, 심지어는 식민시기에 입법된 법규들에 이르기까지 아래와 같은 여러 법규에 산재되어 있으나,

산업재해보상법(Workmen's Compensation Act, 1923)

임금지급법(Payment of Wages Act, 1936)

휴가 및 휴일법(Leave and Holiday Act,1951; 2014년 일부개정)

공장법(Factories Act, 1951; 2016년 일부개정)

상점 및 시설법(Shops and Establishments Act, 1951; 2016년 개정)

유전(노동 및 복지)법[Oilfields(Labor & welfare) Act, 1951]

사호보장법(Social Security Act, 1954)

광산 법령(Mining Rules, 1996)

해외고용법(Law relating to Overseas Employment, 1999)

현재 발효중인 노동관련 주요 법규는 대부분 2013년 이후 개정된 것들로, 아래와 같은 법/시행령 및 고시가 그 중심을 이루고 있다:

- 노동분규 조정 법규(Settlement of Labor Dispute Law & Rules, 2011; 2014년 일부개정)
- 고용 및 숙련기술 촉진법(Employment and Skill Development Law of 2013: ESDL)

- 최저임금법(Minimum Wage Law of 2013) 및 최저임금규정(Minimum Wage Bylaw of 2013)
- 임금지불법(Payment of Wages Law 2016)
- 사회보장법(Social Security Law of 2013)
- 노동조직법(Labor Organization Law, 2011.10/11) 및 노동조직법령(Labor Organization Rule, 2012): 노동조합의 조직과 활동을 합법화한 법규
- 최저임금 설정 국가위원회 고시(Notification No.2/2015 of the National Committee for Stipulation of Minimum Wage)
- 노동부 시행령[MoL Order No.84/2015(July 3, 2015)]: 퇴직금 관련 시행령
- 노동부 시행령(MoL Notification No. 1/2015): 근로계약 체결의무 관련 시행령으로 고용시 근로계약 제출 의무는 물론, 노동부 표준 근로계약 사용을 의무화하고 있음.

* 2011년 10월 11일 노동조합법의 발효에 따라, 노동조합(등록의무)과 노동 쟁의는 약 50년 만에 허용되었고, 2015년 말 현재, 약 1,500여 개의 공장단위 기본 노동조합이 존재하고 있다. 2015년 11월 총선 결과, 오랜 군사정권 및 영향력에서 벗어나고자 하는 국민들의 압도적 지지로 2016년 4월 출범한 신정부(민선 2기, 아웅산 수지 여사 중심의 NLD당 집권)는 노동 및 인권, 민족화합 등을 주요 정책으로 선언하고 있는바, 향후 근로자 권익 강화 및 노동 쟁의가 활발하게 진행될 것으로 예상되어, 외국인 투자자의 고용, 근로관계 관련 법규 변화 및 준수에 각별한 주의를 요한다.

B. 고용절차

1. 미얀마 시민

① 5명 이상의 종업원을 고용하고자 하는 고용주는 지방노동위원회에 통보 (고용예정인 노동자의 유형, 숫자, 요건 등 포함)

② 지방노동위원회는 고용주에게 후보자 리스트를 제공

③ 고용주가 고용예정 종업원 선택하여 지방노동위원회에 통보

④ 고용주와 개별 종업원 간 고용계약 체결

⑤ 지방노동위원회에 고용계약 제출 및 승인 신청

* 단, 노동국 허가를 받아 신문공고를 통한 채용도 가능하며, 이 경우는 상기 ①~③요건 면제

* 5인 이하 소수 고용의 경우도 상기 ①~③요건 면제되어 취업알선 업체를 통해 자유롭게
  고용가능(통상, 급여의 2배 수준의 알선료 요구)

2. 외국인(Foreigners)

외국인투자법에 따라 설립된 법인(FIL 기업)은 비숙련직에 대해서는 100% 현지
인으로 고용하여야 하는 반면,

숙련직에 대해서는 아래 비율한도 내에서 외국인 고용이 가능하다:

- 75% (운영후 최초 2년간)

- 50% (운영 3년차~4년차)

- 25% (운영 5년차~6년차)

외국인 숙련공을 고용하고자 하는 FIL 기업은 아래 절차를 따라야 한다:

- MIC에 제출할 투자제안서상에서 필요한 외국인 인력의 숫자를 공개

- MIC 투자허가 취득

- 노동국에 취업허가(Work Permit) 신청(with a copy of MIC 투자허가 사본과 함께
  제출)

- 이민국(Immigration and National Registration Department)에 체류허가(Stay Permit)
  신청(MIC 투자허가 사본과 함께 제출)

비자(Visa)	단수상용비자 (Single business visa)	10주(70일)한도 체류 가능하며 발급후 3개월간 유효 * *cf) 관광비자 유효기간: 4주(28일)*
	복수입국상용비자 (Multiple-entry business visa)	각 방문시마다 10주 한도 체류 가능, 유효기간: 6개월 또는 1년
장기체류허가 (Long-term stay permit)	단수체류허가 (Single stay permit):	재입국 없이 3개월 또는 1년간 취업가능 갱신 가능
	복수입국허가 (Multi re-entry permit):	유효기간 중 해외여행기간 포함 1년간 미얀마 취업가능(갱신 가능)

• 우리나라와 미얀마 간에 비자 면제 협정이 체결되지 않은 관계로 관광이든 상용이든 미얀마 대사관을 통한 비자 발급이 필요하다. 단, 관용여권의 경우는 무비자로 90일간의 체제가 가능하다.

• 장기체류허가 신청을 위해서는 복수입국비자가 필요함.

• 3개월 이상 체재 외국인은 외국인 등록 필요.

• 외국인 근로자는 10주 상용비자를 취득하고 입국후, 1년간 유효한 장기체류비자(연장가능)를 취득하는 절차를 경유하게 되며, 장기체류허가를 신청하기 위해서는 해당 기업이 관련된 산업에 대한 관할 정부부처 장관 추천서를 첨부하여야 한다.

C. 고용 및 숙련기술 촉진법(ESDL)상 업무지침

1. 고용계약(Employment Contracts)

ESDL 및 노동부 시행령 1/2015(MoL Notification No. 1/2015)에 따라, 채용후 30일 이내에 고용주와 근로자는 고용계약을 체결하여야 하고, 고용주는 체결된 계약을 지방노동청(Township Labor Office; TLO)에 제출하여, 승인을 받아야 한다.

단, 아래는 예외로 한다.

- 고용주가 정부 부서인 경우
- 훈련 및 견습기간 중의 훈련/견습생

또한, 동 시행령에 따라, 노동부는 2015년 9월 2일자로 발표한 표준 근로계약양식을 의무적으로 사용할 것을 모든 고용주에게 요구하였다.

따라서 이에 위반한 경우(해당 근로자가 표준계약 서명을 거부한 경우를 제외), 고용주는 ESDL법에 따라 1년 이하의 징역 또는 (and/or) 벌금형에 처해질 수 있음을 유의할 필요가 있다. 표준계약이 공장 근로자 권익보호를 위해 개발된 것임에도, 지방노동청은 공장뿐만 아니라 모든 산업영역에 일괄 적용을 강제하고 있으나, 현장 실무관행 조사내용에 따르면, 개별 지방노동청 및 담당관에 따라 실무 적용 및 해석상 상당한 차이가 있는 것으로 보인다. 따라서 향후 추가 시행령 및 실무지침 등에 따라 구체화될 때까지는 상기 시행령에 따른 요건과 절차를 최대한 준수하고, 표준계약 조건에 대한 수정/추가 조항이 불가피한 경우(근로자에게 더 유리한 조건을 제공하기 위해)에는, 표준계약에 대한 별첨 등의 방식으로 보완하는 것이 바람직하다.

ESDL법에 따라, 고용주는 각 근로자의 월급여의 0.5%를 숙련기술 촉진기금(Skills and Development Fund)으로 납부하여야 하며, 이 금액은 해당 근로자의 급여에서 공제하여서는 안 된다.

2. 근로 기본 조건

(a) 임금(Wages)

① 최저임금(Minimum Wages):

2013년 개정된 최저임금법 및 최저임금 규정에 따라,
최저임금 협의 및 설정을 위해 구성, 운영된 3자간 국가위원회(정부대표, 고용주협회대표 및 산별노조 대표로 구성)는 2015년 6/29일자로 새로운 최저임금률을 확정, 발표하였고, 2015년 9/1부터 아래와 같은 최저임금이 발효, 의무화되었다

(Notification No.2/2015 of the National Committee for Stipulation of Minimum Wage):

- 일일 최저임금 3,600 짯(Ks) (일일 8시간 기준, 시간당 450Ks):
  (예외)
  - 15명 이하 고용규모의 영세 기업 또는 가족운영 기업의 경우에는 상기 최저 임금의 적용이 면제되나, 상호 합의된 임금률에 따른 근로계약 체결의무
  - 고용주와 배우자 또는 동거중인 친족 관계 근로자에게도 적용 면제

- 법정 최저 일당의 50%인 1,800ks(8시간기준, 시간당 225ks): 미숙련공으로 신규 채용되어 훈련기간 중에 있는 근로자의 경우 최대 3개월 범위 내 적용

- 법정 최저 일당의 75%인 2,700ks(8시간 기준, 시간당338Ks): 신규 고용되어 3개 월 수습기간 중에 있는 근로자의 경우

② 임금/급여 구조

기본급(Basic pay)	
잔업수당 (Overtime charges)	기본급의 200%(초과시간단위 산정)
휴일특근 수당 (Holiday charges)	기본급의 200%(초과일단위 산정)
보너스(Bonus)	법규상 의무조항은 없고, 실무상 일반적으로 매년 기본급(월급)의 100%~200%

* 상점 및 기타 비제조 시설에 종사하는 관리자는, 상점 및 시설 법의 적용이 명시적으로 배제되어, 잔업수당 혜택이 적용되지 않는다.

(b) 법정 근로일 및 근로시간

	공장법	상점 및 시설법	유전법
법정 근로시간	8시간/일	8시간/일	8시간/일
주당 최대 근로시간	44시간 * 48시간 - 기술적 이유로 지속 가동이 요구되는 현장	48시간	44시간 * 48시간 - 기술적 이유로 지속 가동이 요구되는 현장

* 5시간 지속근무 후 30분 휴식 제공

(c) 법정 휴가 및 휴일

정규휴가 Casual Leave	6일 · 특별한 경우 외는 1회에 최대 3일까지 사용가능 · 정규휴가는 다른 휴가와 결합될 수 없음 · 정규휴가는 해당 연중 사용하지 않으면 소멸함
연차휴가 Earned Leave	10일(최초 1년 근속 후 발생) 최대 3년까지 누적
병가 Medical Leave	30일 · 6개월 근무 후 사유 발생시, 급여 100% 지급 · 6개월 이내 사유 발생시, 무급 휴가 허여 가능 · 병가는 연차휴가와 결합사용 가능. 해당 연중 사용되지 않으면 소멸
출산 휴가 Maternity Leave	출산 전 6주, 출산 후 최소 8주(총 14주); 쌍둥이 추가 4주 · 병가와 결합가능
국경일 Public Holidays	정부가 공표한 국경일은 휴무, 일반적으로 연간 약 21일

* 상기 휴가 및 휴일 외에, 고용주와 근로자 간 상호 합의에 따른 추가 유급휴가 가능.

* 무급휴가는 고용주의 승인하에 허여 가능.

(d) 해고 및 퇴직금

① 사직(Termination by Employee)

근로자는 아래와 같이 근로계약을 중도 해약할 수 있다:

(i) 수습기간 중은, 고용주에 대한 7일 전 통보

(ii) 그 외 정규근무 기간 중은, 30일 전 통보

② 해고(Termination by Employer)

(i) 귀책 해고(징계해고)

- 노동부 표준 근로규칙에 규정된 중대 위반행위(절도, 도발, 영업기밀 유출 등)를 저지른 종업원은 퇴직금 지불 없이, 그 위반현장에서 즉시 해고할 수 있다.

- 과실 또는 경미한 (근로규칙) 위반행위의 경우에는, 3회의 공식적인 경고를 받은 후에도 시정되지 않는 경우, 퇴직금 없이 해고할 수 있다.

* 1차, 구두 경고 — 2차, 서면 경고 — 3차, 해당 종업원이 서명한 최종 경고.

(ii) 임의해고(Termination without cause)

종업원의 위반행위 없이 고용주가 고용계약 기간 중 임의로 해고하고자 하는 경우에는 아래 기준에 따른다.

• 수습기간 중: 1개월 사전통보 및 1개월 수습 월급 지급

• 정상근로 기간 중: 1개월 사전통보 및 아래 기준에 따른 퇴직금 지급

[노동부 명령 No.84/2015(2015.7.3)에 따른 퇴직금 기준(개정)]

근속기간	퇴직금(월 기본급 기준)
6 개월 이상 ~ 1년 미만	0.5개월
1년 이상 ~ 2년 미만	1개월
2년 이상 ~ 3년 미만	1.5개월
3년 이상 ~ 4년 미만	3개월
4년 이상 ~ 6년 미만	4개월
6년 이상 ~ 8년 미만	5개월

8년 이상 ~ 10년 미만	6개월
10년 이상 ~ 20년 미만	8개월
20년 이상 ~ 25년 미만	10개월
25년 이상	13개월

* 지방노동청은 근로계약기간 중 해고는 물론, 근로계약 종료 후 갱신 거부의 경우에도 고용주는 상기 퇴직금 지불의무가 있다는 의견을 보이는 경향임에 유의.

X. 외환관리
Foreign Exchange Control

외환거래는 외환관리법(Foreign Exchange Management Law: FEML, 2012)과 외환관리규정(Foreign Exchange Management Regulations: FEMR, 2014)에 따른 통제를 받으며, 중앙은행법에 따라, 미얀마 중앙은행(Central Bank of Myanmar: CBM)이 외환관리법에 따른 관리 및 운영을 담당하고 있다.

과거 우리나라나 대부분 후진국 및 개발도상국들에서와 마찬가지로,

일반적으로 내국인, 외국인 또는 기업을 막론하고, 외화 현찰 또는 외화 증서를 통한 지불, 상환, 차입, 송금, 예탁 및 외화계좌 개설 등 외환거래를 하고자 하는 경우에는 반드시 외환관리원(Foreign Exchange Management Board: FEMB)의 사전 허가를 받아야 한다.

그러나 외국인 투자법상 투자허가를 받아 설립된 법인의 경우에는 외국인 투자법상 투자 과실 및 이익 송금이 허용된다.

중앙은행의 사전 승인이 있는 경우를 제외하고, 외환의 매입/매도, 차입/대차, 송금 및 환전은 반드시 승인받은 환전소(authorized dealer)를 통해 거래하여야 한다.

중안은행의 허가가 있는 경우 외에는, 상기 외환관리법규를 직접 또는 간접으로

위반하거나, 그 적용을 회피할 우려가 있는 모든 계약은 무효가 됨을 유의하여야 한다.

과거 공식환율, 공정환율, 암시장(black market)환율 등으로 나누어 복잡하였던 환율제도는 2012년 4월 시장환율 제도 도입과 공식환전소 허가에 따라 전면 폐지되었다. 현재, 미얀마는 관리변동환율(managed floating rate) 제도를 택하고 있는바, 중앙은행과 승인된 환전소/환전취급 은행들 간의 경매방식을 통해 결정된다. 즉, 환율이 외환시장의 수급현황에 따라 변동되도록 허여하되, 중앙은행이 적정하다고 판단하는 수준에서 환율 안정을 위해 수시로 외환시장에 개입하여 환율수준을 관리하는 환율제도로서, 고정환율제도와 자유변동환율 제도의 장점을 살린 중간 형태라 할 수 있다.

2016년 5월 11일 현재 중앙은행 기준 환율은 USD 1 = 1,168Ks 수준이다. (본격 개방 직전인 2011년 5월 기준 공식환율 1$ = 5.63Ks)

2013년 미국, 유럽 등 서방국가들의 대 미얀마 경제제재 완화 이후, 미국 달러화를 제외한 유로화, 엔화 등 주요화폐의 미얀마 송금은 별다른 제약없이 가능하며,

달러화의 경우, 미국이 2013년 2월 SDN(Specially Designated Nationals: 특별지정 제재대상 리스트로서 이러한 개인, 기업/기관이 지분 50% 이상을 보유한 기관/단체와 미국인/기업의 거래 금지)에 등재되었던 미얀마 4개 은행에 대한 제재를 철회함에 따라,

현재는 국방부 소유 2개 은행(Inwa Bank, Myawaddy Bank)과 국영은행인 Myanmar Foreign Trade Bank(MFTB)를 제외한 모든 미얀마 은행과의 달러화 금융거래가 가능하다.

* 은행예탁 관련, 2016년 5월 11일 기준 중앙은행 기준 이율은 연 10%, 융자

(loan) 최고 이율 연 13%, 최저 예탁(deposit) 이율 8% 수준이고 현지은행들의 저축예금 상품 이율은 8.5%~10% 수준이나 저축예금이나 융자 혜택은 현지인과 기업들에게만 적용되고, 외국인과 외국기업에게는 적용되지 않고 있다. 특히 외국인/기업은 토지 소유나 부동산에 대한 저당 설정권이 허여되지 않는 관계로 현지 은행을 통한 융자는 사실상 불가능한 실정이다.

XI. 부동산
Real Property

미얀마가 군정시절 도입했던 사회주의 경제체제의 영향으로, 아직도 헌법(Union Constitution of 2008) 규정상 모든 토지는 원칙적으로 연방정부 소유인 것으로 규정되어 있어,

현재까지 외국인은 토지를 매입, 소유할 수 없고, 2011년 이전에는 부동산 임대조차도 1년 이내의 단기임대로 제한되어 있었으나, 2011년 9월 발표된 외국인 투자법 시행령(39/2011)에 따라, 장기 임대가 가능하게 되었다. 현재는 외국인 투자법(2012.11)에 따른 MIC 투자허가 법인은 최장 70년(50년+10년 2회 연장권), 경제특별구역법에 따라 허가된 법인에게는 최장 75년(50년+25년 연장권)까지 임대가 가능하게 되었다.

부동산 양도제한법(Transfer of Immovable Property Restriction Act of 1987: TIPA)상으로는 외국인의 토지, 건물 등 부동산 소유 금지는 물론 임대조차도 1년 이내로 제한되어 있어,
(i) 외국인 투자법에 따라 MIC 투자허가를 득하거나,
(ii) 특별경제구역법에 따라 투자허가받은,

외국인 법인의 경우에만 예외적으로 정부기관[또는 정부기관으로부터 장기 임대받은 미얀마 시민(법인)으로부터의 재임대(sublease)]으로부터 장기 임대가 가능하다.

또한, 최근 콘도미니엄법 시행에 따라, 콘도미니엄 건물의 40% 이내 가구 범위 내에서, 6층 이상 객실에 대한 외국인 매입 및 소유가 허여되었다.

한편, 미얀마 등기법(Myanmar Registration Act)에 따르면, 1년을 초과하는 기간 동안의 부동산 임대계약은 관할 등기소(Office of Registration of Deeds: ORD)에 계약체결 후 4개월 이내에 등기하여야 할 의무가 있음을 유의 바란다(1년 이하 임대는 선택적 등기 사항이므로 등기의무 없음).

위의 V. 세무편에서 설명한 바와 같이, 부동산 임대계약에는 인지세(stamp duty)가 부과된다.

XII. 지적재산권
Intellectual Property Rights

특허, 디자인, 상표/상호, 저작권 등 지적재산권 보호관련, 현재 미얀마에서는 일부 식민시절 제정된 오래전 법규가 있으나 이후 폐지 또는 사문화되었거나, 관련 등록 등에 대한 구체적인 규정, 절차가 존재치 않거나, 이를 담당할 전담 조직이 없는 등의 이유로, 지적재산권에 대한 법적 보호나 집행은 사실상 불가능한 상황인지라,

- 특허와 디자인 관련, 그나마 영국 식민시절 제정되었던 1939년의 특허 및 디자인법은 1946년 무렵 폐지에 따라, 현재는 특허와 디자인 관련 법규는 공백 상태.
- 저작권 관련해서는 앤틱화된 1914년 저작권법이 있으나, 저작권 등록등에 관한 절차나 규정이 존재치 않고, 관련한 판례나 소송도 발생한 사례조차 없는 것으로 알려져 있음. 영업비밀 관련해서도 마찬가지로 관련 판례나 재판 사례가 존재치 않음.
- 상표/상호 관련해서는 현재까지 별도의 법규가 제정된 적이 없음.
- 또한, 지재권 등록/관리 관청(상표/특허청 등), 특허법원 또는 전담 재판부 등과 같은 지적재산권 관련 전담 또는 전문 기구도 없음.

유명회사의 위조/유사 상표를 부착한 전자제품, 의류 및 기타 용품 등은 물론, 불법 복제된 음악, 영화 CD/DVD 등이 대형 백화점등에서도 판매되고 있고, 컴퓨터 프로그램 등 소프트웨어의 경우, 오히려 정품 구입/설치 사례를 찾기 힘들다.

그러나 미얀마의 열악한 전력, 정보통신망 및 그로 인한 제조역량 낙후로 인해 주요 첨단 제품 등에 대한 지적재산권 침해에 따른 피해는 극히 제한적인 수준에 머무르고 있다(정보통신/생활가전 제품 등 거의 모든 공산품은 인접한 중국, 태국, 베트남 등으로부터 수입).

미얀마는 WTO의 창립회원국이며(1995년 가입), WIPO(세계 지적재산권기구)의 회원국(2001년 가입)으로 지적재산권 보호의무가 있으나, 최빈국(the least developed nation)으로 분류되어 2013년까지 지재권보호 협약(TRIPs: Agreement on Trade-Related Aspects of Intellectual Property Rights) 준수 의무의 이행을 유예받았으나, 현재까지도 지재권 보호 입법을 못하고 있는 상태이다.

- 이후, WTO는 미얀마 등 최빈국에 대한 TRIPs 협약 이행의무를 2021년까지 유예하였음.
- WIPO 등의 지원하에, 과학기술부가 새로운 지적재산권 법규 초안(특허, 산업 디자인, 저작권 및 상표권 등 4개 법안)을 작성하여, 수년째 정부 내부에서 검토 중이나, 아직 의회에 공식 상정되지 못하고 있는 상황임.

XIII. 연방정부 구성

2008년 연방 헌법(2011년 1월 31일 발효)에 따른 미얀마연방 정부 구성 및 행정구역은 아래와 같다.

A. 입법부

[연방의회] PYIDAUNGSU HLUTTAW (Union Assembly)	**상원** *Amyotha Hluttaw*(National Parliament) • 총 의석: 224명 - *각 지방(Region, State)별 선거 12명 + 군부 선임 4명*
	하원 *Pyithu Hluttaw*(People's Parliament) • 총의석: 440명 - *타운십 / 인구비례 선거 330명 + 군부 선임 110명*
[지방의회]	**지방 의회** Region and State *Hluttaws* • 타운십별, 대의원 2명 • 민족별 회의(연방 총인구의 0.1% 기준, 단, 해당 지방 다수민족은 제외), 대의원 1명 • 군부 선임 대의원: 총 의석의 25%

B. 행정부

대통령		
국방안보위원회 (Nat'l Defence & Security Council) 대통령 부통령 (2) 상원의장 하원의장 총사령관 부사령관 국방장관 외무장관 내무장관	**연방정부** (Union Government) 대통령 부통령(2) 각 부처 장관 법무장관 (Attorney General)	**재정위원회** (Financial Commission) 대통령 부통령(2) 법무장관 감사원장(Auditor-General) 지방 장관(각 지방/주) 네피도 시의장 재무장관 * 연방 및 지방 정부 예산 입안/심사/의회 제안

- 대통령은 국민이 직접 선거를 통해 선출한 의원으로 구성된 의회를 통해 선출되는 간접선거 방식으로 5년 임기

- 상원, 하원 및 군부(군 총사령관이 지명)에서 각 1명의 부통령을 선출하고, 이들 3명의 부통령 중 1명을 연방의원으로 구성된 선거인단에서 대통령으로 선출하는 방식

C. 사법부

최고법원 (최종심)	군사법원 Courts- Martial	연방 대법원 Supreme Court 대법원장 + 대법관 6~10명	헌법재판소 Constitutional Tribunal 재판소장 + 재판관 8명
지방법원 (항소심)		고등법원 High Courts (각 지방 또는 주별 구성) 고등법원장 + 고등법관 2~6명	
기초법원	자치지역 법원 Courts of Self Administered Areas 타운십 법원		지구 법원 District Courts

D. 행정구역

헌법상 미얀마 연방은:

- 7개 Region(버마족 중심 지방),
- 7개 State(버마족 외 소수민족 중심 지방) 및
- Union Territories(직할영역으로 현재는 네피도 1개 지역이나, 필요에 따라 입법에 의거 대통령이 직접 통제하는 연방령 지정 가능)으로 구성되고,

상기 각 지방(Region 및 State)하에는 District, Township, City/Town 등의 하부 행정지구가 존재함.

No.	State/Region	Districts	Townships	Cities/ Towns	Wards	Village groups	Villages
1	Kachin State	4	18	20	116	606	2630
2	Kayah State	2	7	7	29	79	624
3	Kayin State	3	7	10	46	376	2092
4	Chin State	2	9	9	29	475	1355
5	Sagaing Region	8	37	37	171	1769	6095
6	Tanintharyi Region	3	10	10	63	265	1255
7	Bago Region	4	28	33	246	1424	6498
8	Magway Region	5	25	26	160	1543	4774
9	Mandalay Region	7	31	29	259	1611	5472
10	Mon State	2	10	11	69	381	1199
11	Rakhine State	4	17	17	120	1041	3871
12	Yangon Region	4	45	20	685	634	2119
13	Shan State	11	54	54	336	1626	15513
14	Ayeyarwady Region	6	26	29	219	1912	11651
	Total	65	324	312	2548	13742	65148

E. 2016년 신정부 부처 현황(2016년 5월 10일 기준)

2016년 4월, 이전 연방정부하의 36개 부처에서 21개 부처로 축소 · 개편하여 출범하였으나, 5월 10일자로 1개 부처 추가하여 현재 22개 부처 존재

부 처	
Ministry of Agriculture, Livestock and Irrigation	
Ministry of Border Affairs	군 총사령관 지명권
Ministry of Commerce	
Ministry of Construction	
Ministry of Defense	군 총사령관 지명권
Ministry of Education	
Ministry of Electric Power and Energy	
Ministry of Ethnic Affairs	
Ministry of Foreign Affairs	
Ministry of Health	
Ministry of Home Affairs	군 총사령관 지명권
Ministry of Hotels and Tourism	
Ministry of Industry	
Ministry of Information	
Ministry of Labour, Immigration and Population	
Ministry of Natural Resources and Environmental Conservation	
Ministry of Planning and Finance	
Ministry of Religious Affairs and Culture	
Ministry of Social Welfare, Relief and Resettlement	
Ministry of Transport and Communications	
Ministry of the President's Office	
Ministry of the State Counselor's Office	2016.5.10 추가 승인
독립부서(준 부처)	
State Counselor	국무총리기능과 유사
Union Auditor General	
Union Attorney-General	

부 록

1. 외국인 투자법(2012.Nov.2) [영문본]
(Foreign Investment Law of 2012; No 21/2012)

2. 외국인투자법 기본시행령(2013.Jan.31) [영문본]
(MNPED Notification No. 11/2013)

3. 외국인 투자허가(MIC PERMIT) 신청서 및 부속서류

4. 법인(외국인회사) 등록 신청서 및 부속서류

5. 미얀마 특별경제구역법(2014.Jan.23) [영문본]
(Special Economic Zones Law)

6. 국영기업법(1989.Mar.31) [영문본]
(State-Owned Economic Enterprises Law)

부록 1

THE FOREIGN INVESTMENT LAW
(THE PYIDAUNGSU HLUTTAW LAW NO 21/2012) (THE 3rd WANING OF THADINGYUT, 1374 ME) (2ND NOVEMBER, 2012)

The Pyidaungsu Hluttaw hereby enacts this Law.

CHAPTER (I)
Title and Definition

1. This law shall be called **the Foreign Investment Law**.

2. The following expressions contained in this Law shall have the meaning given hereunder:
   (a) **Union** means the Republic of the Union of Myanmar;
   (b) **Commission** means the Myanmar Investment Commission formed under this Law;
   (c) **Union Government** means the Union Government of the Republic of the Union of Myanmar;
   (d) **Citizen** includes an associate citizen or a naturalized citizen. In this expression, an economic organization formed with only citizens shall also be included by this Law;
   (e) **Foreigner** means a person who is not a citizen. In this expression, an economic organization formed with foreigners shall also be included by this Law;
   (f) **Promoter** means any citizen or any foreigner submitting a proposal relating to an investment to the Commission;
   (g) **Proposal** means the stipulated application submitted by a promoter to the Commission for approval of an intended investment accompanied by draft contract, financial documents and company documents;
   (h) **Permit** means the order in which the approval of the Commission relating to

the proposal is expressed;

(i) **Foreign Capital** includes the followings which are invested in the business by any foreigner under the permit:

(i) foreign Currency;

(ii) property actually required for the business and which is not available within the Union such as machinery, equipment, machinery components, spare parts and instruments;

(iii) rights which can be evaluated the intellectual property such as license, patent, industrial design, trademark, copyright;

(iv) technical know-how;

(v) re-investment out of benefits accrued to the business from the above or out of share of profits;

(j) **Investor** means a person or an economic organization invested under the permit;

(k) **Bank** means any bank permitted by the Union Government within the Union;

(l) **Investment** means various kinds of property supervised by the investor within the territory of Union under this Law. In this expression, the followings shall be included:

(i) right to be mortgaged and right to mortgage in accord with law on the rights relating to the movable property, immovable property and other property;

(ii) shares, stocks and debentures of the company;

(iii) financial rights or activities under a contract as a value relating to the finance;

(iv) intellectual property rights according to the existing Laws;

(v) functional rights granted by the relevant law or contract including the rights for exploration and extraction of natural resources;

(m) **Person entitled as land leaser or land user** means the person who is entitled to lease land or the person who is entitled to use land until the stipulated period by paying stipulated leasing rate for such land to the Union.

CHAPTER (II)
APPLICABLE BUSINESS

3. This Law shall apply to business stipulated by the Commission, by notification, with the prior approval of the Union Government.

4. The following investments shall be stipulated as the restricted or prohibited business:
   (a) business which can affect the traditional culture and customs of the national races within the Union;
   (b) business which can affect the public health;
   (c) business which can cause damage to the natural environment and ecosystem;
   (d) business which can bring the hazardous or poisonous wastes into the Union;
   (e) the factory which produce or the business which use hazardous chemicals under international agreements;
   (f) manufacturing business and services which can be carried out by the citizens by issuing rules;
   (g) business which can bring the technologies, medicines, instruments which is testing in abroad or not obtaining the approval to use;
   (h) business for farming agriculture, and short term and long term agriculture which can be carried out by citizens by issuing rules;
   (i) business of breeding which can be carried out by citizens by issuing rules;
   (j) business of Myanmar Marine Fisheries which can be carried out by citizens by issuing rules;
   (k) business of foreign investment to be carried out within 10 miles from borderline connecting the Union territory and other countries except the areas stipulated as economic zone with the permission of the Union Government.

5. The Commission may allow by the approval of the Union Government, the restricted or prohibited investments under section 4 for the interest of the Union and citizens especially people of national races.

6. The Commission shall, the foreign investment business which can cause great effect on the conditions of security, economic, environmental and social interest of

the Union and citizens, submit to the Pyidaungsu Hluttaw through the Union Government.

CHAPTER (III)
AIM

7. Aimed at the people to enjoy sufficiently and to enable the surplus to export after exploiting abundant resources of the country; causing to open up of more employments for the people as the business develop and expand; causing to develop human resources; causing to develop infrastructures such as banking and financial business, high grade main roads, highways roads connected one country to another, national electric and energy production business, high technology including modern information technology; causing to develop respective area of studies in the entire country including communication networks, transport business such as rail, ship, aircraft which meet the international standard; causing the citizens to carry out together with other countries; causing to rise economic enterprises and investment business in accord with the international norms.

CHAPTER (IV)
BASIC PRINCIPLES

8. The investment shall be permitted based on the following principles:
   (a) supporting the main objectives of the economic development plan, business which cannot be affordable and which are financially and technolo-gically insufficiency by the Union and its citizen;
   (b) development of employment opportunities;
   (c) promotion and expansion of exports;
   (d) production of Import substituted goods;
   (e) production of products which require mass investment;
   (f) acquisition of high technology and development of manufacturing business by high technology;
   (g) supporting the business of production and services involving large capital;

(h) bringing out of business which would save energy consumption;

(i) regional development;

(j) exploration and extraction of new energy and the emergence of renewable energy sources such as bio-basic new energy;

(k) development of modern industry;

(l) protection and conservation of environment;

(m) causing to support for enabling to exchange the information and technology;

(n) not affecting the sovereign power and the public security;

(o) intellectual enhancement of citizens;

(p) development of bank and banking in accordance with the international standards;

(q) emergence of the modern series required for the Union and citizens;

(r) causing to be sufficient the local consumption of the energy and resources of the Union in terms of short term and long term period.

CHAPTER (V)
FORM OF INVESTMENT

9. The investment may be carried out in any of the following forms:

(a) carrying out an investment by a foreigner with one hundred per cent foreign capital on the business permitted by the Commission;

(b) carrying out a joint venture between a foreigner and a citizen or the relevant Government department and organization;

(c) carrying out by any system contained in the contract which approved by both parties;

10. (a) In forming the form of investment under section 9:

(i) shall be formed as company in accord with the existing law;

(ii) if it is formed as a joint venture under sub-section (b) of section 9, the ratio of foreign capital and citizen capital may be prescribed in accord with the approval of both foreigner and citizen who has made joint venture;

(iii) in investing by the foreigner, the Commission shall, the minimum amount of investment according to the sector, prescribe with the approval of the Union Government depending on the nature of business;

    (iv) the foreigner may, if a joint venture is carried out with citizen in prohibited and restricted business, propose the ratio of the foreign capital as prescribed by the rule;

(b) In carrying out the form of investment business under sub-section (a), liquidating before the expiry of the term of the contract as it has obtained the right to terminate or liquidating on the conclusion of the business shall be complied with and exercised in accord with existing laws of the Union.

CHAPTER (VI)
FORMATION OF THE COMMISSION

11. (a) The Union Government shall

    (i) in respect of investment business, form the Myanmar Investment Commission with a suitable person from the Union level as Chairman, the experts and suitable persons from the relevant Union Ministries, Government departments, Government organizations and non-Governmental Organizations as members for enabling to carry out the functions and duties contained in this Law;

    (ii) in forming the Commission, stipulate and assign duty to the Vice-Chairman, the Secretary and the Joint Secretary out of the members;

(b) Members of Commission who are not civil service personnel shall have the right to enjoy salary, allowances and recompense allowed by the Ministry of National Planning and Economic Development.

CHAPTER (VII)
DUTIES AND POWERS OF THE COMMISSION

12. The duties of the Commission are as follows:

(a) taking into consideration on the facts such as financial credibility, economic justification of the business, appropriateness of technology and protection and conservation of environment in scrutinizing the proposals of investment whether or not the proposal is in conformity with the principles of Chapter 4 of this Law;

(b) taking prompt action as necessary if the investors complain that they do not enjoy the rights fully which are entitled under the Law;

(c) scrutinizing whether or not the proposals are contrary to the provisions of the existing laws;

(d) submitting performances to the sixth-monthly meeting of the Pyidaungsu Hluttaw through the Union Government;

(e) submitting advice to the Union Government, from time to time, to facilitate and promote local and foreign investments;

(f) prescribing the category of investment, value amount of investment and term of business with the prior permission of the Union Government and altering thereof;

(g) coordinating with the relevant Region or State Government in respect of foreign investments which are entitled to carry out for economic development of the Regions or State with the approval of the Union Government;

(h) administering to know immediately and to take action by the Commission if it is found that the natural resources or antique object which is not contained in the original contract and it is not applied with the allowed business above and under the land which has the right to use;

(i) scrutinizing whether or not the investment business is abided by in accord with this Law, rules, regulations, by-laws, procedures, orders, notifications and directives made under this Law, the matters contained in the contract by the investor; if it is not abided by, causing to abide by it and taking action against the business in accord with the law;

(j) prescribing the investment business which is not required to grant exemption and relief from tax;

(k) performing duties as are assigned by the Union Government from time to time;

13. The powers of the Commission are as follows:

(a) accepting the proposal which is considered beneficial to the interests of the Union and which is not contrary to any existing law after necessary scrutinizing;

(b) issuing permit to the promoter or the investor if the proposal is accepted;

(c) allowing or refusing the extension or amendment of the terms of the permit or the agreement if it is applied by those concerned after scrutinizing in accord with the stipulations;

(d) requesting to submit necessary evidence or facts from the promoter or the investor;

(e) passing any necessary order to the extent of the suspension of business if the sufficient evidence has appeared that the investor does not abide by and carry out in accord with the proposal submitted to the Commission to obtain the permit, the instruments and evidence attached to it or the terms and conditions contained in the permit;

(f) allowing or refusing the bank which is proposed by the promoter or the investor to carry out financial matters;

14. The Commission may, in performing and implementation of their duties, form committees and bodies as may be necessary.

15. The reports on the performance of the Commission shall be submitted at the meeting of the Union Government from time to time.

16. Conditions on the completion and improvement of the business permitted by the Commission shall be reported to the third-monthly meeting of the Union Government.

CHAPTER (VIII)
DUTIES AND RIGHTS OF THE INVESTOR

17. The duties of an investor are as follows:

(a) abiding by the existing Laws of the Republic of the Union of Myanmar;

(b) performing the business activities by incorporating a company under the existing Laws of the Republic of the Union of Myanmar by investor;

(c) abiding by the provisions of this Law, terms and conditions contained in the rules, procedures, notifications, orders, directives and permits issued under this Law;

(d) using the land which he is entitled to lease or use in accord with the terms and conditions stipulated by the Commission and those contained in the agreement;

(e) carrying out to sub-lease and mortgage the land and building which are allowed to carry out business under the permit, transfer the shares and the business to any other person for such investment business within the term of the business only with the approval of the Commission;

(f) making no alteration of topography or elevation of the land obviously on which he is entitled to lease or use without the approval of the Commission;

(g) informing immediately to the Commission if natural mineral resources or antique objects and treasure trove which are not related to the permitted business and not included in the original contract are found above and under the land on which he is entitled to lease or use, continuing to carry out business on such land if the Commission allows, and transferring and carrying out to the substituted place which is selected and submitted by the investor if the permission of continuing to carry out is not obtained;

(h) carrying out not to cause environmental pollution or damage in accord with existing laws in respect of investment business;

(i) in case of a foreign company, if all of the shares are absolutely sold and transferred to any foreigner or any citizen, registering the transfer of share in accord with the existing law only after returning the permit with the prior permission of the Commission;

(j) in case of a foreign company, if some of its shares are absolutely sold and transferred to any foreigner or any citizen, registering the transfer of share in accord with the existing law only after obtaining the prior approval of the Commission;

(k) carrying out the systematic transfer of high technology relating to the business which are carried out by the investor to the relevant enterprises, departments or organizations in accord with the contract;

18. The rights for the investor are as follows:

(a) entitle to sell, exchange or transfer by any other means of assets with the approval of the Commission according to the existing laws;

(b) in case of a foreign company, selling all or some of its shares absolutely to any foreigner/any citizen or any foreign company/any citizen company;

(c) carrying out the expansion of investment business or increasing of foreign capital contained in the original proposal by obtaining the approval of the Commission;

(d) submitting to the Commission to re-scrutinize and amend in order to obtain the rights which he is entitled to enjoy fully in accord with the existing law;

(e) applying to the Commission for obtaining benefits and for taking action in respect of the grievance in accord with the existing laws;

(f) applying to the Commission to obtain more benefits for the invention of new technologies, the enhancement of product quality, the increase in production of goods and the reduction of environmental pollution in investment business carried out under the permit;

(g) being entitled to enjoy the period stipulated by the Commission with the approval of the Union Government, more than the period of tax exemption and tax relief contained in Chapter(XII), for the investors who invest in foreign investment in the regions which are less developed and difficult to access for the development purpose in the entire Nation.

CHAPTER (IX)
APPLICATION FOR PERIT

19. An investor or a promoter shall, if it is desirous to make foreign investment, submit a proposal to obtain a permit to the Commission in accord with the stipulations.

20. The Commission:

(a) may accept or refuse the proposal within 15 days after making necessary scrutiny if the proposal submitted under section 19 is received;

(b) shall allow or refuse the proposal within 90 days to the person who submit the proposal if the proposal is accepted;

21. If the investor or the promoter obtains the permit issued by the Commission, an investment shall be established after concluding necessary contract with the relevant Government department and organization or person and organization.

22. The Commission may, if it is applied by those concerned, allow the extending, reducing or amending of the term or agreement contained in the contract as appropriate in accord with this Law.

CHAPTER (X)
INSURANCE

23. The investor shall insure the stipulated types of insurance with any insurance business allowed to carry out within the Union.

CHAPTER (XI)
APPOINTMENT OF STAFF AND WORKERS

24. The investor shall:
   (a) in appointing skilled citizen workers, technicians and staff for skilled jobs, citizens shall have been appointed at least 25 percent within the first two-year, at least 50 percent within the second two-year and at least 75 percent within the third two-year from the year of commencement of the business. Provided that the Commission may increase the suitable time limit for the business based on knowledge;
   (b) to be able to appoint under sub-section (a), arrange to provide practicing and training to citizen staff for improvement of the working skills;
   (c) appoint only citizens for the works which do not require skills;
   (d) carry out the recruitment of workers from the Labour Exchange Office or local labour exchange agencies or by the arrangement of the investor;
   (e) appoint skilled citizen workers, technicians and staff by signing an employment agreement between employer and workers in accord with the existing labour laws and rules;

(f) administer the rights of causing not to differ the level of wages in appointing the Myanmar citizen staff like the foreign staff as the allocation of expert level.

25. The foreigners who work at the investment business under the permit shall submit and apply for the work permit and the local residence permit issued by the Union.

26. The investor shall:
  (a) conclude an employment agreement in accord with the stipulations in appointing staff and workers;
  (b) carry out to enjoy the rights contained in the existing labour laws and rules including minimum wages and salary, leaves, holiday, overtime fee, damages, workman's compensation, social welfare and other insurance relating to workers in stipulating the rights and duties of employers and workers or the occupational terms and conditions contained in the employment agreement;
  (c) settle the disputes arisen among employers, among workers, between employers and workers and technicians or staff in accord with the relevant existing laws;

CHAPTER (XII)
EXEMPTIONS AND RELIEFS

27. The Commission shall, for the purpose of promoting foreign investments within the State, grant the investor the tax exemption or the relief contained in Sub-section (a) out of the following tax exemptions or tax reliefs. In addition, one or more than one or all of the remaining tax exemptions or tax reliefs may be granted if it is applied:
  (a) income tax exemption for a period of five consecutive years including the year of commencement on commercial scale to any business for the production of goods or services, moreover, in case where it is beneficial to the Union, income tax exemption or relief for suitable period depending upon the success of the business in which investment is made;

(b) exemptions or reliefs from income tax on profits of the business if they are maintained for re-investment in a reserve fund and re-invested therein within 1 year after the reserve is made;

(c) right to deduct depreciation from the profit, after computing as the rate of deducting depreciation stipulated by the Union, in respect of machinery, equipment, building or other capital assets used in the business for the purpose of income tax assessment;

(d) if the goods produced by any manufacturing business are exported, relief from income tax up to 50 percent on the profits accrued from the said export;

(e) right to pay income tax on the income of foreigners at the rates applicable to the citizens residing within the Union;

(f) right to deduct expenses from the assessable income, such expenses incurred in respect of research and development relating to the business which are actually required and are carried out within the Union;

(g) right to carry forward and set-off the loss up to 3 consecutive years from the year the loss is actually sustained within 2 years following the enjoyment of exemption or relief from income tax as contained in sub-section (a), for each business;

(h) exemption or relief from custom duty or other internal taxes or both on machinery, equipment, instruments, machinery components, spare parts and materials used in the business, which are imported as they are actually required for use during the period of construction of business;

(i) exemption or relief from customs duty or other internal taxes or both on raw materials imported for production for the first three-year after the completion of construction of business;

(j) if the volume of investment is increased with the approval of the Commission and the original investment business is expanded during the permitted period, exemption or relief from custom duty or other internal taxes or both on machinery, equipment, instruments, machinery components, spare parts and materials used in the business which are imported as they are actually required for use in the business expanded as such;

(k) exemption or relief from commercial tax on the goods produced for export;

CHAPTER (XIII)
GUARANTEES

28. The Union Government guarantees that a business formed under the permit shall not be nationalized within the term of the contract or the extended term if such term is extended.

29. The Union Government guarantees not to suspend any investment business carried out under the permit of the Commission before the expiry of the permitted term without any sufficient cause.

30. On the expiry of the term of the contract, the Union Government guarantees the investor invested in foreign capital to disburse his rights in the category of foreign currency in which such investment was made.

CHAPTER (XIV)
RIGHT TO USE LAND

31. The Commission may allow the investor actually required period of the right to lease or use land up to initial 50 years depending upon the category of the business, industry and the volume of investment.

32. The Commission may extend the period of consecutive 10 years and for further 10 years after the expiry of such period to the investor desirous of continuation of the business after the expiry of the term permitted under section 31, depending upon the volume of investment and category of business.

33. The Commission may, for the purpose of economic development of the Union, allow to make investment on such land by obtaining the initial agreement from the person who is entitled to lease or use land with the prior approval of the Union Government.

34. The Commission may, from time to time, stipulate in respect of rates of rent for

the land owned by the Government departments and organization with the prior approval of the Union Government.

35. The investor has the right to carry out, in performing the contract system of agricultural and breeding business in farms, only by joint venture system with citizen investors which are allowed to carry out by the citizens.

36. The Commission may, for the purpose of the development of the entire Nation, stipulate longer than the period for the right to lease or use land contained in this Law, for enjoyment of the investors who has invested in the region where the economy is less developed and difficult to access with the approval of the Union Government.

CHAPTER (XV)
FOREIGN CAPITAL

37. The foreign capital shall be registered with the name of the investor in the category of foreign currency accepted by the bank by the Commission. The category of foreign capital shall be mentioned in such registration.

38. In the event of termination of business, the person who has brought in foreign capital may withdraw foreign capital which he may withdraw as prescribed by the Commission within the stipulated time.

CHAPTER (XVI)
RIGHT TO TRANSFER FOREIGN CURRENCY

39. The investor has the right to transfer abroad the following foreign currency through the bank which has the right to carry out foreign banking within the Union in the relevant foreign currency at the stipulated exchange rate:
　(a) foreign currency entitle to the person who has brought in foreign capital;
　(b) foreign currency permitted for withdrawal by the Commission to the person

who has brought in foreign capital;

(c) net profit after deducting all taxes and the relevant funds from the annual profit received by the person who has brought in foreign capital;

(d) legitimate balance, after causing payment to be made in respect of taxes and after deducting in the manner prescribed, living expenses incurred for himself and his family, out of the salary and lawful income obtained by the foreign staff during performance of service in the Union;

CHAPTER (XVII)
MATTERS RELATING TO FOREIGN CURRENCY

40. The investor shall:

(a) be transferable abroad through any bank within the Union which has the right to carry out foreign banking in the relevant foreign currency at the stipulated exchange rate;

(b) carry out financial matters relating to the business by opening a foreign account in the category of foreign currency accepted by the bank within the Union which has the right to carry out foreign banking or a kyat account.

41. The foreigners serving in any economic organization formed with the permit shall open a foreign account in the category of foreign currency accepted by the bank within the Union which has the right to carry out foreign banking or a kyat account.

CHAPTER (XVIII)
ADMINISTRATIVE PENALTIES

42. The commission may pass the following one or more administrative penalties against the investor who violates any of the provisions of this Law, rules, regulations, by-laws, procedures, notifications, orders, directives issued under this Law or terms and conditions mentioned in the permit:

(a) censure;

(b) temporary suspension of tax exemption and relief;

(c) revocation of the permit;

(d) black listed with no further issuance of any permit in the future;

CHAPTER (XIX)
SETTLEMENT OF DISPUTES

43. If any dispute arises in respect of the investment business:

    (a) dispute arisen between the disputed persons shall be settled amicably;

    (b) if such dispute cannot be settled under sub-section (a):

        (i) it shall be complied and carried out in accord with the existing laws of the Union if the dispute settlement mechanism is not stipulated in the relevant agreement;

        (ii) it shall be complied and carried out in accord with the dispute settlement mechanism if it is stipulated in the relevant agreement.

CHAPTER (XX)
MISCELLANEOUS

44. The Commission may, after producing to fulfill the required energy for the Union and citizen by aiming to export the exceeding energy to abroad, scrutinize and allow if the investor submits the proposal to make investment under the production sharing system or enjoying the allocation on obtaining the profits between the Union Government or Government department and organization conferred power by the Union Government in accord with the law and the investor for feasibility study, exploration, survey and excavation and carrying out to reach the production level on commercial scale at the stipulated site within the stipulated period by using the investor's capital fully in the production such as petroleum and natural gas, mineral which require mass capital employing a joint venture with the Union or citizen in accord with this Law. If such investment business is commercially feasible, the profit shall be entitled to enjoy proportionately between the Union Government or Government department and organization conferred

power by the Union Government in accord with law or citizen and the investor who works in joint-venture to cover the profit.

45. The investor under the Union of Myanmar Foreign Investment Law (The State Law and Order Restoration Council Law No. 10/1989) before the promulgation of this Law shall be deemed as investors stipulated under this Law.

46. If the credible evidence is appeared that the investor intentionally make false statement or conceal the accounts, instruments documents, financial documents, employment documents attached to the proposal prepared and submitted to the Commission, relevant Government department and organization, he shall be taken action under criminal proceeding.

47. Notwithstanding anything contained in any existing law, matters relating to any provision of this Law shall be carried out in accord with this Law.

48. The commission shall hold meetings in accord with the stipulations.

49. The decision of the Commission made under the powers conferred by this Law shall be final and conclusive.

50. No suit, criminal proceeding or other proceeding shall lie against any member of the Commission, committee or body or any civil service for any act done in good faith which has credible evidence in accord with the power conferred under this Law.

51. To enable to carry out the provisions of this Law, the Ministry of National Planning and Economic Development or any organization shall:
    (a) take responsibility and carry out the office-works of the Commission;
    (b) incur the expenditures of the Commission;

52. The investor who is carrying out by the permit of the Commission under the Union of Myanmar Foreign Investment Law (State Law and Order Restoration Council, Law No.10/1988) which is to be replaced by this Law shall be entitled to

proceed and enjoy continuously until the expiry of the term in accord with terms and conditions contained in the permit and the relevant agreement.

53. The Commission shall, in permitting the foreign investment business under section 3 and section 5 if it affects the interest of the Union and citizen, submit to the nearest Pyidaungsu Hluttaw session through the Union Government as the important matters.

54. If any provision of this law is contrary with any matter of the international treaty and agreement adopted by the Republic of the Union of Myanmar, the matters contained in the international treaty and agreement shall be abided by.

55. After prescribing this Law, within the period before prescribing the necessary rules and regulations, the rules and regulations issued under the Union of Myanmar Foreign Investment Law (The State Law and Order Restoration Council, Law No. 10/1988) may be continued to exercise if it is not contrary with this Law.

56. In implementing the provisions of this Law:
   (a) the Ministry of National Planning and Economic Development shall, with the approval of the Union Government, issue rules, regulations and by-law, procedures, orders, notifications and directives as may be necessary within (90) days from the adoption of this Law;
   (b) the Commission may issue orders, notifications and directives as may be necessary.

57. The Union of Myanmar Foreign Investment Law (The State Law and Order Restoration Council, Law No. 10/1988) is hereby repealed by this Law.

I hereby sign under the Constitution of the Republic of the Union of Myanmar.

sd/ Thein Sein President
Republic of the Union of Myanmar

Government of the Republic of the Union of Myanmar Ministry of National Planning and Economic Development Notification No. 11/2013
The 5th Waning Day of Pyatho, 1374 ME (31st January, 2013)

In exercise of the power conferred under sub-section (a) of Section 56 of the Republic of the Union of Myanmar Foreign Investment Law (Law No. 21 of Pyidaungsu Hluttaw, 2012), the Ministry of National Planning and Economic Development has prescribed these Rules with the approval of Union Government:

Chapter I
Title and Definition

1. These Rules shall be called the Foreign Investment Rules.

2. The expressions contained in these Rules are to have same meaning contained in the Foreign Investment Law. Moreover, the following expressions shall have the meanings given hereunder:
   (a) **Ministry** means the Ministry of National Planning and Economic Development.
   (b) **Commission Office** means Directorate of Investment and Company Administration which is responsible to implement the duties and responsibilities of Myanmar Investment Commission.
   (c) **Director General** means Director General of the Directorate of Investment and Company Administration.
   (d) **Form** means the form stipulated in these Rules.
   (e) **Schedule** means the schedule prescribed in these Rules.
   (f) **BOT** means Building, Operating and Transfer from the business operator to the relevant person at the expiry of the contract term.
   (g) **BTO** means Building, Transfer from the business operator to the relevant person after the building and operating the business.
   (h) **Asset** means land, building, vehicles and other asset relating to the business.

In this expression share, bond and other similar instruments are also included.

Chapter II
Applicable Economic Activities

3. The Commission shall issue the Notification and designate the economic activities applicable to the Foreign Investment Law with the approval of the Union Government. In doing so it shall base on the following criteria:
   (a) labour intensive industry with the view to create employment opportunities for the citizens;
   (b) business which enables to produce value added of products of the Union;
   (c) business which is capital intensive industry;
   (d) business applying high technology;
   (e) business producing goods and services which focuses on to causing the welfare of consumption of citizens;
   (f) business which supports to promote the living standard of the citizens;
   (g) business which support the technology and increase the capital for the small and medium enterprises operated by citizens.

4. The Commission shall submit and obtain approval from the Union Government for the designation of investment businesses which are categorized by prohibited business for investment within the Union, investment business only to form joint - venture with citizens and investment business only permitted with the specific condition.

5. After obtaining the approval from the Union Government, the Commission shall issue the Notification for the prohibited business for investment within the Union, investment business only to form joint-venture with citizens and investment business only permitted with the specific condition.

6. The Commission may amend the changes of designated businesses for the benefit of the Union and its citizens especially for the benefit of indigeneous groups

of the people of the Union with the prior approval of the Union Government.

7. The manufacturing and service businesses which are enable to carry out by the citizens are prescribed in the **Schedule I**.

8. The agricultural businesses and short term and long term plantation businesses which are enable to carry out by the citizens are prescribed in the **Schedule II**.

9. The livestock breeding businesses which are enabling to carry out by the citizens are prescribed in the **Schedule III**.

10. The fishing businesses at the Myanmar's territorial waters which are enabling to carry out by the citizens are prescribed in the **Schedule IV**.

11. The Commission may, from time to time, amend the designated businesses prescribed according to the Rules 7, 8, 9 and 10 by submitting to the Pyidaungsu Hluttaw through the Union Government.

12. The Commission may designate the combined zones of manufacturing and service businesses including industrial zones, tourism zones, trade zones, located within 10 miles from the border lines between the Union and its neighbouring countries as Economic Zones by submitting to the Union Government.

13. Designation of Economic Zones prescribed under Rule 12, the Commission shall submit and obtain the permission from the Union Government when the Union Government has given instruction or proposed by the Government of relevant Region or State or by the leading body of Self-Administered Division or Self-Administered Zone, or proposed by the investor or developer with the approval of the Government from the relevant Region or State or the leading body of Self- Administered Division or Self-Administered Zone upon the proposal of the investor or developer.

14. The Commission shall, when the foreign investor has proposed to carry out the investment business which is restricted or prohibited, for the benefit of the Union

and its citizens especially for the benefit of the indigenous groups of people of the Union, scrutinize based on the following criteria:

(a) comments of the local people or social organizations of the relevant location upon the proposed investment;

(b) comments of the local administrative bodies of the relevant location upon the proposed investment;

(c) comments of the Nay Pyi Taw Council or the Government of relevant Region or State or the leading body of Self-Administered Division or Self-Administered Zone depending on the relevant location where the investment business is to be carried out;

15. Commission shall submit and obtain the approval from the Union Government for the investment proposals which are completed with the requirements stated in the Rule 14 together with its own comment.

16. Commission shall issue the permit for the foreign investment to the promoter or the investor after getting the approval of the Union Government.

Chapter III
Form of Investment

17. The investment may carry out in any of the following forms:

(a) carrying out with one hundred percent foreign capital by the foreigner in other business except for the businesses prescribed with the Notification issued by the Commission under Rule 5;

(b) carrying out the capital contribution of foreigner and citizen by concluding the contract in accord with the mutual agreement if it is formed as a joint-venture between a foreigner and a citizen or the relevant government department and organization;

(c) carrying out in various forms of cooperation systems between the Government and private including BOT system, BTO system or other system according to any system of Contractual Agreement;

2. 외국인투자법 기본시행령 **117**

18. The application for the establishment or the registration as a foreign company according to the existing Company Law shall be applied to the Directorate of Investment and Company Administration together with the submitting of foreign investment proposal.

19. The Director General of the Directorate of Investment and Company Administration has the right to issue the Certificate of Incorporation (temporary) and Form of Permit (temporary) if the promoter or investor has requested to issue in advance. However, issuance in advance of the Certificate of Incorporation (temporary) and Form of Permit (temporary) is not meant to the permission for the investment.

20. The maximum foreign investment capital ratio shall not be more than eighty percent of the total investment amount if the foreigner has formed joint-venture with the citizen to carry out prohibited or restricted businesses. The Commission may amend the said stipulation by issuing notification from time to time with the approval of the Union Government.

21. The liquidation of business shall obtain prior approval from the Commission when obtain the right to terminate before the expiry of term of contract or after completion of the business activities and shall be abided by the existing Companies Act.

Chapter IV
Formation of the Commission and Convening the Meeting

22. The Commission shall be formed more than nine members and shall have odd number.

23. The term of each Commission member shall not exceed three years. However, the Union Government may assign the Commission member for more than three years when it is required for expertise and other requirements.

24. If one of the members of the Commission cannot fulfill the duty before three year tenure, the term of the assigned successor for that vacancy shall be same as the remaining term of the predecessor.

25. The Commission shall convene the meetings at least twice a month.

26. The Commission Chariman shall act as a Chairman of the meeting. The Vice-Chairman or Secretary or one of the Commission members shall chair the meeting when the Chairman or Vice- Chairman or both of them are not available.

27. The quorum of the meeting shall meet more than 50 percent of the Commission members.

28. The Commission shall make the decision by the conformity of more than fifty percent of the members who have attended the Commission meeting. The decision made by these attended Commission members at the meeting shall not be objected, denied or amended by the Commission members who are not present.

29. The Commission, carrying out its duties prescribed in these Rules shall be implemented with transparency, responsibility, accountability and fair competition among the investors with the view to clear vision of the people including the investors. The Commission shall prevent from the monopoly investment.

30. The Commission may, if necessary, invite relevant Ministry, Union Minister or Deputy Minister, technical experts and other relevant persons to the meeting.

31. The Commission shall allow the promoter or investor and their supporting persons for investment to attend and make explanations and discussions at the meetings.

Chapter V
Application for the Permit

32. The investor or the promoter shall, in submitting proposal, fill the **Proposal Form (1)** by completing the following particulars and signed by the promoter or investor:

   (a) name of investor or promoter, citizenship, address, business location, actual operating business in accord with the relevant law, location of head office of effective management, location of incorporated business organization, type of business;

   (b) facts contained in clause (a) related to person desirous to join in the joint-venture if the investment is formed as joint-venture;

   (c) documents related to the clause (a) or (b);

   (d) business and financial documents of the investor, promoter or a person desirous to join in the joint-venture;

   (e) facts related to manufacturing or service business desirous to invest;

   (f) duration of investment and construction period;

   (g) location of investment business in the Union;

   (h) technical know-how to be used for the production and system of sales;

   (i) type and volume of energy consumption;

   (j) quantity and value of required main machinery, equipments, raw materials and similar materials to be used in business during the construction period;

   (k) required area and type of land;

   (l) estimated amount and value of the annual production or service to be carried out from the business;

   (m) annual required foreign currency expenditure for business and estimated foreign currency income;

   (n) estimated amount, value and period of annual sales of products in local and export;

   (o) condition of economic justification;

   (p) measures for conservation and prevention plan for the environmental and social impacts according to the provisions of the relevant existing law;

   (q) form of investment in the Union;

   (r) if desirous to form partnership, the draft contract, share ratio and amount of the shares to be contributed by the partners, ratio for allocation of profit and duties and responsibilities of the partners;

(s) if desirous to form limited company, draft contract, draft memorandum of association and articles of association, authorized capital of the company, type of shares, amount of share to be contributed by the shareholders;

(t) name, citizenship, address and designation of the directors for the investment organization;

(u) total paid up capital of the investment organization, ratio of local and foreign capital contribution and total foreign capital brought in and brought in period into the Union;

(v) undertaking to follow the terms of the contract;

33. Draft land lease contract to be signed with citizen or government departments, organizations and draft contract related to business for the joint-venture or by mutual contract shall be submitted together with the investment proposal.

34. In submitting the proposal for the capital intensive investment projects designated by the Commission and designated businesses which need to assess the environmental impact by the Ministry of Environmental Conservation and Forestry, the environmental impact assessment and social impact assessment reports shall be attached together with the investment proposal.

35. In submitting the proposal which is natural resource-based investment businesses and investment under the State-owned Economic Enterprises Law, shall be submitted to the Commission through the relevant Union Ministry.

36. The investor or promoter shall submit the proposal directly to the Commission office for the investment businesses which are not related to the condition mentioned in the Rule 35.

37. The Commission Office shall scrutinize after receiving the proposal submitted under Rule 36, whether the stipulated facts are completed in accord with the requirements and accept the complete proposal. If the investment proposal is not completed, the investor or promoter shall be requested to resubmit by completing

the requirements.

38. The Commission shall form the Proposal Assessment Team to scrutinize the completed proposals respectively with the senior officials from the following departments:
    (a) Directorate of Investment and Company Administration;
    (b) Customs Department;
    (c) Internal Revenue Department;
    (d) Directorate of Labour;
    (e) Relevant Department under the Ministry of Electric Power;
    (f) Department of Human Settlement and Housing Development;
    (g) Department of Industrial Supervision and Inspection;
    (h) Directorate of Trade;
    (i) Project Appraisal & Progress Reporting Department;
    (j) Department of Environmental Conservation;

39. The technicians and experts from the relevant organizations and departments are invited to attend for the preliminary scrutiny under Rule 37, as may be necessary.

40. The Director General is responsible as a team leader of the Proposal Assessment Team.

41. The Proposal Assessment Team shall convene the meeting once a week to make assessment on the proposals received before the meeting period and the acceptable proposals shall be submitted to the Commission in accordance with the Rules. If the proposal is approved or declined by the Commission, the approval or reasons of decline shall be informed to the investor or promoter by mail or any other means of communication systems.

42. The Proposal Assessment Team shall invite the promoter or the investor or the authorized person on behalf of the promoter or the investor to attend the meeting.

Chapter VI
Processing upon the Proposal

43. The Commission Office shall request when the Commission has accepted the proposal, the recommendations from the Nay Pyi Taw Council or relevant Region or State Government upon the investment proposal whether the proposal is acceptable or not and recommendation upon the measures to protect or minimize the environmental and social impacts from the Ministry of Environmental Conservation and Forestry.

44. The Nay Pyi Taw Council or Region/State Government shall reply the recommendation letter signed by Chairman of the Nay Pyi Taw Council or Chief Minister of the relevant Region/State Government or a responsible person on behalf of Chief Minister whether the investment proposal is acceptable or not based on the necessary scrutiny, to the Commission by within seven days from the date of request letter was received.

45. The Ministry of Environmental Conservation and Forestry shall reply the recommendation letter by scrutinizing the measures for protection or minimization of environmental and social impacts, signed by Union Minister or responsible personnel on behalf of the Union Minister by any speedy communication means within seven days from the date of request letter was received.

46. The relevant Ministries shall reply, their recommendations within seven days from the date of request letter was received, to the Commission when the Commission has requested the recommendations or advisory remarks on the investment proposal in accordance with the nature of business or requirement. The relevant Ministry shall form the Investment Assessment Response Team headed by Director or same rank with the Director as a minimum level to reply the request. The relevant Ministry shall instruct the adopted investment policies with regard to the specific area to the said team. The information of the Investment Assessment Response Team and every change of the member shall be informed to the Commission. The team, on behalf of the relevant Ministry, shall attend the meeting conducted by Commission or Commission Office when it is invited from time to time.

47. The Commission Office shall submit the proposal to the upcoming nearest Commission meeting when the relevant recommendations and assessments are received.

Chapter VII
Scrutinizing of Proposal

48. The Commission shall carry out the investment proposals as follows:
   (a) scrutinizing as to whether or not the proposal complies with the basic principles stated in Chapter IV of the Foreign Investment Law;
   (b) requesting and scrutinizing the following facts for the financial credibility;
     (i) Bank Statement;
     (ii) latest audit report of the company;
     (iii) performance report of the company;
   (c) scrutinizing the economic justification based on the following facts:
     (i) estimated annual net profit;
     (ii) estimated annual income and expenditure in terms of foreign currency;
     (iii) investment recoupment period;
     (iv) new employment opportunities;
     (v) contribution to national income and tax generation;
     (vi) market access for domestic and export;
     (vii) local consumption requirement;
   (d) assigning technicians and experts for the assessment of appropriateness for relevant industrial technology, innovation and transfer of technology;
   (e) scrutinizing the recommendation on the measures for conservation and protection of impacts to environmental and social aspects by the Department of Environmental Conservation;
   (f) scrutinizing for accountability to the Union and citizens and emphasizing on the socio-economic benefits;
   (g) scrutinizing the proposal whether it is abided in accordance with the provisions of the existing laws;

Chapter VIII
Issuing Permit

49. The Commission shall scrutinize the proposal and if it is accepted, the **Permit Form (2)** shall be issued within 90 days from the date of receipt. The copies of the Permit shall be sent to the relevant Union Ministries.

Chapter IX
Procedure after the Approval

50. The investor or promoter shall, after receiving the permit from the Commission, complete the construction process within the period of construction or extended period if so. The completion of the construction shall be informed to the Commission within 30 days soon after it was completed.

51. The investor shall commence the production or services after the completion of the construction period.

52. The **Report Form (3)** of its own business shall be submitted to the Commission once in every three months by mail or by any other means of communication system during the permitted operation period of the investment business.

53. The promoter or investor shall inform immediately to the relevant Head of Township Administration Department and the Commission within 24 hours by any possible way of communications in case of facing any condition as per Rule 124 during the business operation.

54. If the business of the promoter or investor is necessary to obtain the license or permit from the relevant Union Ministries, Government Departments and Organizations according to the nature of investment business or other requirements; or necessary to register, it shall be continued to carry out in accord with the stipulations.

55. The promoter or investor shall:
   (a) abide by the Environmental Conservation Law for the environmental conservation activities with regard to the business;
   (b) implement the business to be responsible investment causing beneficiary and accountability for the Union and citizens;
   (c) cooperate with the responsible personnel for the inspection to the business from time to time or according to necessity;
   (d) carry out seriously according to the standards adopted by the relevant Union Ministries for the construction of factory, workshop, building and other business activities and to be in line with the business performances;
   (e) provide safety work environment and health programme in the work site;
   (f) abide by the regulations, procedures and standards adopted by the relevant Union Ministries for the transportation, storage and usage of hazardous and toxic materials and other similar materials;
   (g) carry out the products produced from the investment business according to the quality or standards with the view not to harm the consumers;

56. The Commission, in accordance with the Notifications, Orders, Directives, Procedures, may allow amendment for the following applications within fifteen days:
   (a) application for the expansion of original proposed investment business or increasing of investment capital by getting permission of the Commission;
   (b) application to the Commission to obtain all the eligible exemptions and reliefs entitled to the investor by scrutinizing and making amendment;
   (c) application to the Commission for getting benefits according to the existing laws or taking action for the grievances;

57. The Permit issued for the mineral exploration shall not be related with the any business of feasibility study or extraction. The investor shall obtain the permission from the Commission through the Ministry of Mines after completion of the mineral exploration to continue the feasibility study and extraction of the minerals.

Chapter X
Stipulation of Construction Period

58. The investor shall carry out to complete the construction works within the stipulated construction period from the date of issuing permit after receiving the permit issued by the Commission.

59. The investor shall, if the construction activities are not completed within the stipulated construction period due to various causes, request for extension of the construction period at least 60 days in advance before the expiry date of stipulated construction period to the Commission with the explanation for the delay.

60. The Commission may, if the investor requests for extension of construction period, after necessary inspections, approve the extension of construction period not longer than 50 percent of the original construction period upon request of the investor based on the inspection of reasonable circumstances for extension.

61. The extension for the construction period shall not be allowed more than twice except the conditions of force majeure such as natural disasters, instabilities, riots, and strikes, a State of emergency, armed opposition, rebellion, and outbreak of wars.

62. The construction period shall be stipulated according to the terms and conditions of the contract by the permission of the Commission for the surveying and feasibility study of exploration, extraction, upgrading and operation for the production of commercial scale of the oil, gas and minerals.

63. The Commission shall withdraw the permit issued to the investor if the construction process is not completed within the original permitted construction period or extended construction period. There is no liability for the reimbursement of remedy, compensation or any other rights or financial terms to the investor due to withdrawal of the permit.

Chapter XI
Lease, Mortgage, Transfer of Share and Transfer of Business

64. The investor shall carry out only obtaining the permission after applying to the Commission Office within the permitted term for the permitted leased land and building without any changes of the type of business with the permission from the person who has the right to use the land or right to lease the land with the **Lease Form (4)** for sub-lease or **Mortgage Form (5)** for mortgage. If the type of land is vacant, fallow or virgin land the permission from the Union Government shall be attached and submitted.

65. The Commission Office shall scrutinize the following facts when receiving the application by the stipulated forms under the Rule 64:
   (a) the reason for lease or mortgage is true or not;
   (b) lease or mortgage without prejudice to the interests of the Union and the citizens;
   (c) capacity of the transferee to continue and accomplish the business successfully;

66. The Commission Office may accept or refuse by the findings of the scrutiny in accordance with the decision of the Commission after submitting the nearest Commission meeting.

67. If desirous to sell all shares completely to any foreigner or citizen shall be applied to the Commission Office after completing the **Share Transfer Form (6)**. In applying so, the person who sells of shares shall attach the recommendation letter of the Head of the relevant Tax and Revenue office by stating clearance according to the scrutinizing to the share transfer application. The permission of the Union Government shall be attached if the investment business made on the vacant, fallow and virgin land.

68. The Commission Office shall scrutinize the following particulars when the application with stipulated form under Rule 67 is received:
   (a) the reason for transfer of all shares is true or not;

(b) transfer of all shares without prejudice to the interests of the Union and the citizens;

(c) capacity of the transferee to continue and accomplish the business successfully;

69. The Commission Office may submit to the nearest Commission meeting that the transfer of all shares should be permitted under scrutiny if it is deemed to allow or refuse in accordance with the decision of the Commission.

70. The person who sells all shares shall return the permit to the Commission Office.

71. If the share transferee is a foreigner, may apply the right of establishment or registration as foreign company to the Directorate of Investment and Company Administration in accord with the existing Company Act or if the share transferer agrees, may continue to use the name of the existing company.

72. If the share transferee is a citizen, shall apply the Permit to the Commission in accord with the Myanmar Citizens Investment Law. After obtaining the permit of Commission, it shall be registered as Myanmar Citizen Company at the Directorate of Investment and Company Administration in accord with the existing Company Act.

73. In issuing the new Permit, the share transferee is entitled to continue to enjoy for the remaining of the allowed period of term if the original investor has remained to enjoy exemptions and reliefs stated under the Chapter XII of Foreign Investment Law, exemptions and reliefs under section 27. Such exemptions and reliefs shall not be enjoyed again for issuing the new Permit if the stipulated period is over.

74. If desirous to transfer completely some of the shares to any foreigner or citizen shall apply to the Commission after completing the **Share Transfer Form (7)**.

75. The Commission Office shall scrutinize the followings, when the application by

stipulated form is received under Rule 74:

(a) the reason of transfer of some of the shares is true or not;

(b) transfer of some of the shares without prejudicing the interests of the Union and the citizens;

(c) capacity of the transferee to continue and accomplish the business successfully;

76. The Commission Office may submit to the nearest Commission meeting if it is considered that the transfer of some of the shares should be permitted based on the scrutiny and allow continuing to carry out or refuse in accord with the decision of the Commission.

77. If the permission is obtained, along with the permit of the Commission, the transfer of shares shall be applied and registered at the Directorate of Investment and Company Administration in accord with the existing Company Act.

78. In performing the scrutiny of Rules 65, 68 and 75, the Commission Office has the right to form the Scrutiny Body as may be necessary by comprising the experts from relevant government departments and organizations by the permission of the Commission.

Chapter XII
Insurance

79. The permitted enterprises shall insure the following types of insurance at any insurance enterprise which is entitled to carry out the insurance activities within the Union:

(a) Machinery Insurance;

(b) Fire Insurance;

(c) Maritime Insurance;

(d) Insurance for Disabling Accident;

(e) Insurance for Natural Disaster;

(f) Life Insurance;

80. Any other form of insurance under any existing laws, regulations and procedures according to the types of business including the types of insurance stipulated as per Rule 79 shall be insured.

Chapter XIII
Employment of Staff and Labour

81. The investor, when submitting the proposal, the number of skilled labours, experts and staff to be employed for skillful jobs and number of unskilled labour, shall be identified.

82. The recruitment of citizen experts, skilled labours and staff shall be appointed for the skillful jobs as per section 24 of the Chapter XI of the Law when the business is operated in commercial scale. The wages and salary shall not be lower than the stipulated minimum wages and salary according to the relevant existing laws, rules, regulations, notifications, orders, directives and procedures.

83. The Commission shall issue Notification of the basic principles for the list of businesses which require to recruite for experts, technicians and staffs with citizens and the changes of time schedule for the business based on knowledge.

84. The investor shall follow the existing Labour Laws in recruiting the staff and labours.

85. The investor shall conclude the employment agreement within 30 days from the date of appointment of staff and labours for citizens and foreigners in accord with the instruction of Ministry of Labour, Employment and Social Security.

86. The investor shall submit the annual plan to the Commission Office before 31st January annually in respect of practicing and training for capacity development of the citizen staff.

87. The investor shall apply the certificate of work permits with the **Work Permit**

Form (8) for the foreign staff and labours working in the permitted investment business with the recommendation of the Commission to the Ministry of Labour, Employment and Social Security according to the Foreign Labour Law. The certificate of stay permit shall be applied with the **Stay Permit Form (9)** to the Commission Office.

88. The Commission Office shall issue the permit when obtaining the application under Rule 87, scrutinize by the departmental cooperation working group formed with the representatives from relevant departments at the Commission Office.

89. The investor shall register at the Social Security Board to enjoy the rights allowed under the Social Security Law by all of the employees who are receiving either in Myanmar Kyat or foreign currency and working at the departments covers under the Social Security Law.

90. The investor shall register at the relevant Social Security Board within 15 days after the commencement of the business and it shall submit to the Commission Office attached with the copy of registration card issued by the Social Security Board.

91. The investor shall submit the recommendation for the full payment of fees to the Social Security Board issued by the relevant Social Security Office to the Commission Office for enabling to continue to carry out the investment, once every six months.

92. The investor shall submit with the attachment of recommendation from the relevant Social Security Board for the clearance of the full payment when the contract term has expired and before withdrawing all the receivables.

93. The dispute arising between the employer or group of employers and the employee or the group of employees shall be settled under the Settlement of Labour Dispute Law.

94. Regarding the right of entering and stay of foreigners who are relating to the

investment shall be abided by the existing Immigration law, rules, regulations, notifications, orders, directives and procedures.

Chapter XIV
Exemptions and Reliefs

95. The investor or the promoter for enjoying the exemptions and reliefs prescribed in the section 27 (b) to (k) of Chapter XII of the Foreign Investment Law, has the right to apply with the tax exemption and relief **Form (10)** to the Commission to allow to enjoy any exemption or relief, in more or all.

96. The Commission may scrutinize and allow if necessary when the investor or promoter has applied the exemptions and reliefs under Rule 95. In scrutinizing as such, the required evidences and documents may be requested and scrutinized from the investor or promoter or relevant government department and organization or other relevant organization.

97. The commencement date of commercial operation of any manufacturing or service business is determined as follows:
   (a) the date specified on the documents used in Bill of Lading or Airway Bill or similar documents used in international trade for the export of manufacturing business, such date shall not exceed 180 days from the date of completion of the construction period;
   (b) the date of the income first-derived from the local sales of the manufacturing business, such date shall not exceed 90 days from the date of completion of the construction period;
   (c) the date which commence of service business, such date shall not exceed 90 days from the date of completion of the construction period;

98. The investor or promoter shall apply the commencement date of commercial operation with **Report Form (11)** for their manufacturing or service business to the Commission in accord with Rule 97.

99. The Commission may, in allowing for enjoying tax exemptions and reliefs, after scrutinizing based on the application submitted by the promoter or investor, specify and allow the commencement date of commercial operation. Type and enjoying period of tax exemption or relief shall be specified when allowing for enjoying as such. Such permission shall be informed to the promoter or investor and to the relevant Government departments and organizations.

100. The Commission shall issue the necessary notification for the permission of tax exemption or rate of concession according to the type of investment business.

Chapter XV
Right to Use Land

101. The Commission may allow the investor to lease the following types of land for the purpose to carry out any commercial business permitted by the Commission from the person having the right to lease the land or person having right to use the land with the prior approval of the Union Government:

  (a) Land which is entitled to manage by the government;
  (b) Land owned by the government department, government organization;
  (c) Private land owned by citizen;

102. The investor who is desirous to lease for conducting agricultural, livestock breeding business on commercial scale by using the vacant, fallow and virgin lands and work for economic development relating thereof may lease in accord with the Vacant, Fallow and Virgin Lands Management Law.

103. The Commission may allow the investor for the period of leasing the land or using the land up to initial 50 years from a person having the right to lease or use the land in accordance with the actual required period of the right to lease or period of the right to use the land based on the types of business and amount of investment.

104. The Commission may, if the investor desirous to continue to carry out after the expiry of the term of lease permitted to the investor under the section 31 of Foreign

Investment Law and if it is approved by the person having the right to lease the land or the person having the right to use of land, allow to extend two consecutive terms by 10 years each based on investment amount and type of business.

105. The application shall submit to the Central Management Committee of Vacant, Fallow and Virgin Land according to the Vacant, Fallow and Virgin Lands Management Law for the investment of agricultural and livestock breeding business and other related business thereof. In doing so, it may allow initial leasing period of 30 years for the period of right to lease or period of right to use of the vacant, fallow and virgin land for the agricultural and livestock breeding business based on the investment amount as to the provisions of the said Law. For the business desirous to continue to carry out, after the expiry of the permitted term, may be allowed to extend based on the type of business and amount of investment in accord with the Vacant, Fallow and Virgin Lands Management Law.

106. The investor is allowed to form joint-venture with the citizen who has the right to conduct agricultural and livestock breeding in the vacant, fallow and virgin land by contributing suitable ratio of technology and investment capital.

107. The person having the right to lease or use the vacant, fallow and virgin land shall pay the premium prescribed in the Vacant, Fallow and Virgin Lands Management Law and Rules for permitted to lease or use vacant, fallow and virgin land.

108. The investor is only allowed to carry out the contract farming system on the farm land permitted to the citizens by forming joint-venture with the citizen investor who obtained the right to carry out to grow seasonal crops on mutual interest.

109. The investor is allowed to form Joint Venture with the citizen who has the right to conduct agricultural and livestock breeding in the vacant, fallow and virgin land by contributing technology and investment capital with mutually agreed joint venture terms with citizen.

110. The Commission may, for the purpose of all round development of the country, with the prior permission of the Union Government, allow to enjoy extra

land lease period for a maximum of 10 years than the land use term prescribed in Rules 103 and 104 for the persons who invest in the regions which are economically less developed and difficult to communicate.

111. The investor or promoter shall, in respect of land desired to be used for the purpose of carrying out any commercial business, apply to the Commission for obtaining the right to lease land by completing the **Land Lease Form (12)** and attached with documents of ageement by the person having the right to lease land or eligible to use of such land.

112. The Commission shall, if it is applied under Rule 111, request the opinion from Nay Pyi Taw Council, Regional Government or State Government depending upon the location of the operation whether to approve and permit in respect of the land desirous to be used by the applicant.

113. If the land desirous to use is owned or administered by the government department, government organization, the letter addressed to the Commission that the relevant government department, government organization agrees to lease, shall be attached.

114. In processing of land lease after obtaining the permit from the Commission, a person having the right to lease land or use land and the investor shall conclude the land lease agreement and send such agreement to the Commission.

115. The Commission may allow the land lease rates which are approved by the relevant Union Ministries with regard to land lease rate of the land owned by the government department, government organization and may submit to the Union Government, if necessary.

116. With the view to conclude the annual land lease agreement in accord with the land lease rate leased by the investor from the citizen having the right to lease land or use land and the current market price according to the lease period, shall be discussed and determined and submitted the agreed rate of land lease to the Commission.

117. In determination of land leasing rate, it shall base and calculate the rate to be paid for 365 days from the date of commencement of the lease for the lease period.

118. In leasing of Government department-owned land or Government organization-owned land, the relevant government department or government organization may demand for land use premium from the investor.

119. The Commission may, when any one of following conditions in respect of land lease has occurred, terminate the land lease and the business permitted:
   (a) it is found the complaint is true that the investor fails to pay fees of land lease in accord with the term of contract or fails to comply with other terms of the contract upon the submission to the Commission by a person on having the right to lease land or use land after necessary inquiry;
   (b) it is found the complaint is true that the investor violates any existing law on the leased and upon the complaint to the Commission after necessary inquiry;
   (c) the investor is declared black list or, if the court or any organ of power decides to close the business invested and carrying out after it was adjudicated in accord with law due to violation of any existing law;

120. The investor shall:
   (a) If desirous to terminate the business, if it is not comply with the economic justifcation, loss or other reasons, shall submit to the Commission at least six months in advance.
   (b) If the investor finds out natural resources, antique, ancient monument or treasure trove in the vacant, fallow and virgin land for doing agriculture and livestock breeding businesses or other business which is permitted by the government, shall inform within 24 hours from the time of such finding to the Head of relevant township administration office and the Commission.
   (c) Re-transfer the land to a person having the right to lease or use the land within seven days from the date of liquidation by both parties after carrying out in accord with the terms and conditions of the contract concluded by him and a person having the right to lease land and after the completion of the lease.
   (d) If the business is terminated before the expiry of the term of lease agreement by any cause stated in Rule 119 or any other cause, it shall be paid the fees of

lease as the terms prescribed in the original agreement so as not to aggrieve to a person having the right to lease land or use land.

121. The person having the right to lease land or use land shall inform the receipt of the land to the Commission within seven days from the date of receiving back the leased land.

122. The investor is not allowed to do other businesses which are not related to the originally permitted businesses on the leased land.

123. The investor must not extract resources above and under the ground of the land leased by the investor apart from the business permitted by the Commission.

124. If the investor finds natural resource or antique or ancient monument or treasure trove which are not included in the original agreement that is not relating to business permitted, above and underground of the land of which the investor has the right to lease or use shall inform promptly to the Head of the relevant administration office and the Commission within 24 hours from the time of such finding. The Commission may discuss with Union Ministry, Nay Pyi Taw Council or relevant Region or State government based on the location of the business, when it was informed. It may be continued to carry out on such land if the Commission has allowed with the agreement of relevant Union Ministry. If not permitted, it shall move to the place arranged in substitution and carry out.

125. The investor has the right to alter and use the topography or elevation of the land for which the investor has obtained the right of lease or use only with the approval of the relevant Union Ministry or a person having the right to lease or use the land.

126. If it is scrutinized by the Commission that the investor carries out the business on the leased land which is not compatible with the original proposal, shall be terminated or not to continue the permit.

127. The investor does not have the right to carry out any other works except the

works relating to farm crops cultivation and production without the approval of the Union Government in leasing to carry out the farms on which the citizen has obtained the right to carry out in accord with the existing laws.

128. The investor, for operating any business, does not have the right to lease and carry out the following lands:

  (a) religious lands;

  (b) cultural heritage regions, natural heritage region which are designated by the relevant Union Ministries;

  (c) lands restricted for State defense and security;

  (d) lands under litigation;

  (e) lands restricted by the State from time to time;

  (f) place or land where exists building which may cause situation such as impact on public environment, noise, pollution, impact on culture within urban residential area due to the business of the investor.

129. The investor shall use the land which he is entitled to lease or use in accord with the terms and conditions prescribed by the Commission and terms and conditions stated in the contract.

130. If the investment business includes urbanization, hotels, schools, hospitals, construction of residential buildings, building factories, roads and bridges, communications, building infrastructure, it shall be submitted to the Commission and carried out only when it is allowed in accord with the city development plans of the relevant Nay Pyi Taw Council, Government of the Region and State, relevant Development Committee and Government departments, Government organization.

131. The investor shall carry out only when the permission of the Commission is obtained for altering and carrying out other business after terminating the originally proposed business, extending and operating other business in addition to the business originally proposed on the land he has leased.

132. The Central Management Committee of the Vacant, Fallow and Virgin Land shall have the right to claim back the minimum area from the permitted Vacant,

Fallow and Virgin Land if one of the following conditions occurs:

   (a) if the historic cultural resources are found at the permitted vacant, fallow and virgin land;

   (b) if the other mineral resources which are not included originally permitted vacant, fallow and virgin land for the exploration of minerals are found;

133. The Central Management Committee of the Vacant, Fallow and Virgin Land shall coordinate with the relevant government department, government organization to refund the compensation within the appropriate stipulated period after calculating the current value for the actual cost of investment of the person having the right to lease or use of the permitted vacant, fallow and virgin land for taken back under the Rules with the approval of the Union Government.

Chapter XVI
Foreign Capital

134. The investor shall open an account and deposit the foreign currency mentioned in the proposal in accord with the permit of the Commission for any economic business in any bank within the Union which has the right to operate in foreign currency.

135. In proposing to invest, except the appropriated money for the matter proposed for foreign capital assets to be imported into the Union under sub-section i (ii) of Section 2 of the Foreign Investment Law, the matters contained in sub-section i (iii) and (iv) of Section 2 of the Foreign Investment Law, the full foreign currency proposed for local investment or the amount of foreign currency to be invested and used if it is carried out step by step in period of years respectively shall be deposited by opening the account in accord with Rule 134.

136. The investor is entitled to transfer the foreign currency from his bank account for the following matters:

   (a) to be paid in foreign currency in the country;

   (b) for account transfer to the affiliated company business in the country, the citizen or the citizen-owned company business for the matters related to business which he has invested;

137. The investor shall not draw and expend or transfer the foreign currency from his bank account for other matters not related to business that he has invested.

138. The investment capital prescribed in the proposal shall be transferred and remitted from any bank located outside the country.

139. The investor shall prepare amendment as may be necessary of the original projection of foreign currency which was approved by the Commission in respect of the reduction of the amount of the investment and the business and re-submit to the Commission.

140. The investor shall assign to any government recognized audit firm which is registered and carrying out business in the Union by performing regular auditing once in 365 days for each and every invested business. In this regard the audited accounts and documents shall be submitted either in Myanmar Language or English Language. If it is in other language it shall be attached the English version recognized by notary.

141. The investor shall submit the audit report to the Commission within 30 days from the date of receipt of the audit report after audited the account under Rule 140.

Chapter XVII
Right to Transfer the Foreign Currency

142. The investor may transfer the following foreign currency through the bank prescribed by the Commission with the relevant foreign currency to abroad:
  (a) the following foreign currency which should be entitled by the person who has brought in foreign capital;
    (i) the foreign currency permitted to repatriate by the Commission to the person who has brought in the foreign capital;
    (ii) the compensation received by the investor according to the relevant

existing law;

(b) the following foreign currency permitted to repatriate by the Commission to the person who has brought in the foreign capital-

    (i) the share entitled to the foreign investor after transferring the share according to the relevant existing law;

    (ii) the share allotment after the liquidation of the business;

    (iii) the foreign currency entitle to the investor after the expiry and return of the permit issued by the Commission;

    (iv) the equivalent amount of foreign currency due to the reduction of the investment;

(c) net profit after deducting the various taxes relating to relevant funds from the annual profits received by the person who has brought in the foreign capital;

(d) legitimate balance after paying the taxes due and after deducting living expenses for himself and his family in the manner prescribed, out of the salary and lawful income obtained by the foreign service personnel by performing service in the Union;

143. The investor shall, if desirous to transfer the foreign currency which is not payment for current transition, apply with the **Transfer Form (13)** addressed to the Commission attached with the following documents:

    (a) Audit report of the related investment business;

    (b) Bank Statement;

144. According to Rule 143, the Commission may allow to transfer the foreign currency with the same amount as applied or lesser than such amount after scrutinizing for the application submitted by the investor.

145. The investor has the right for account transfer of local currency generated from the business to the Kyat currency account opened at the bank by a citizen or a citizen-owned business in the Union and right to transfer back the equivalent amount of foreign currency from the foreign currency bank account of citizen or citizen-owned business by submitting the sufficient documents.

146. The investor shall, if desirous to extend and invest the business without

transferring the profits obtained from the business invested to abroad, submit to the Commission and obtain permission from the Commission.

147. The investor shall not be allowed to deposit in his account without the permission of the Commission by transferring to the foreign currency from Kyat which is received by selling of any assets invested with the permission of the Commission.

148. The investor shall not be allowed to purchase any foreign capital which is to be remitted from abroad according to the proposal by using Kyat within the Union without the permission of the Commission.

149. The investor shall not pay for expenses to be expended within the Union in terms of Kyat which is received by selling of any assets in the Union imported from abroad according to the proposal for the business invested by him.

150. The foreign capital shall not be entitled to transfer to abroad before the day of commencement of commercial operation of the investment business.

Chapter XVIII
Matters Relating to Foreign Currency

151. The investor:
   (a) is entitled to transfer currency in the relevant foreign currency though any bank which has the right to carry out foreign banking within the Union at the stipulated exchange rate by the Central Bank;
   (b) shall open foreign currency account and Kyat account at any bank which had the right to carry out foreign banking within the Union and carry out financial matters related to business.
   (c) is entitled to exchange any kind of foreign currency accepted by the bank which has the right to carry out foreign banking within the Union obtained in Kyat legally by himself.

152. The foreigners who have employed at investment business shall open foreign

currency account and Kyat account at any bank which has the right to carry out for foreign banking within the Union.

Chapter XIX
Departmental Cooperation Team

153. The Commission shall form the Departmental Cooperation Team comprising the officials from the following departments causing to enhance foreign investment business, to facilitate, for enabling to make field inspection to the business operations and to provide one stop service in accord with section 14 of the Foreign Investment Law:

(a) Central Bank of Myanmar;

(b) Relevant Department from the Ministry of Electric Power;

(c) Directorate of Investment and Company Administration;

(d) Customs Department;

(e) Directorate of Trade;

(f) Department of Labour;

(g) Department of Immigration and National Registration;

(h) Directorate of Industrial Supervision and Inspection;

(i) Internal Revenue Department;

154. The Deputy Director General of the Directorate of Investment and Company Administration shall take responsible as a leader of the Departmental Cooperation Team.

155. The office of the Departmental Cooperation Team shall be opened jointly at the Directorate of Investment and Company Administration office. The branch offices may be formed if necessary.

156. The officials assigned in the Departmental Cooperation Team shall be empowered the right to make decision including the right to sign by the relevant departments. If it arises the matters related to policy, the relevant department shall make a decision promptly upon the submission of the relevant official.

157. The Departmental Cooperation Team shall conduct field inspection and report to the Commission for the progress during the construction period of the permitted business for designation of commercially commencement date and conducting inspection of the implementation of the business.

158. The Departmental Cooperation Team shall serve under the supervision of Director General.

Chapter XX
Administrative Penalties

159. The Commission shall inquire by forming investigation team, if it is inquired, inspected or any complaint, information accrued that the investor does not abide by any provisions contained in the Foreign Investment Law or in these Rules; or obtaining permit by submitting dishonestly the fault information the matters contained in the proposal or found guilty that breaching any regulations and by-law, procedures, notifications, orders, directives or any conditions contained in the permit issued by the Commission.

160. The investigation team shall be formed with the persons who are experts and have fair- minded from the relevant government departments, associations, organizations led by one of the members of the Commission. In forming the investigation team, it shall form with not less than 3 members including the Team leader.

161. The investigation team shall have the right to investigate and asking to the relevant government departments, associations, the persons from the organizations, other persons, for documentary evidence.

162. The investigation team shall submit the findings of inquiry to the Commission within 21 days commencing from the date of issuing order to form the team. The relevant penalty shall be suggested from the administrative penalties stated in section 42 of the Chapter XVIII of the Foreign Investment Law when submitting so.

163. The Commission shall discuss in respect of passing administrative penalty at the meeting. The investor under investigation shall also be allowed to participate and present at that meeting.

164. The effectiveness of the penalty shall be commenced on the date of final decision made by the Commission with regard to the administrative penalties.

Chapter XXI
Settlement of Dispute

165. If any dispute arises between the investor and any individual or government, any government department in respect of the investment business, dispute arisen shall be settled amicably.

166. If the dispute cannot settled according under Rule 165:
   (a) it shall be complied and carried out in accord with the dispute settlement mechanism if it is stipulated in the relevant agreement;
   (b) it shall be complied and carried out in accord with the relevant existing Laws of the Union if the dispute settlement mechanism is not stipulated in the relevant agreement;

167. The investor shall, in expressing the factual basis, inform and submit to the Commission when dispute arises.

168. To resolve the dispute, the investor may file the documents issued by the Commission as evidence if necessary. It is entitled to apply to the Commission for other evidences related to the Commission, if necessary.

169. The investor shall submit and request the permission to the Commission, if the situation arises that any staff from the Commission Office is to appear before the court as witness.

Chapter XXII
Miscellaneous

170. The investor has the right to continue to enjoy the exemptions and reliefs prescribed in the Chapter XII of the Foreign Investment Law if the investor is still enjoying exemptions and reliefs allowed under the Union of Myanmar Foreign Investment Law (State Law and Order Restoration Council Law No. 10/1988) which was superseded by the Foreign Investment Law.

171. The investor who has already been enjoyed the exemptions and relief contained in stipulated period under the Union of Myanmar Foreign Investment Law shall not entitle to enjoy the exemptions and reliefs stated at Chapter XII of the Foreign Investment Law.

172. The investor shall be taken criminal action if the evidence is found that the investor had intentionally made false statement or conceal the accounts, documentary instruments, and financial documents, employment documents attached to the proposal prepared and submitted to the Commission, relevant Government department and organization.

173. The investor who performing investment business according to the Permit issued by the Commission and formed under the Union of Myanmar Foreign Investment Law (State Law and Order Restoration Council Law No. 10/1988) shall apply to the Commission for the continuity to carry out and enjoying the benefits in accord with the conditions prescribed under the Foreign Investment Law.

174. The investments in business of manufacturing or services as non-profit, non-commercial purposes are not subject to these Rules.

175. Business operating solely for trade shall not subject to these Rules.

176. The Commission shall submit the report once every six months of its performances to the Pyidaungsu Hluttaw through the Union Government.

177. The Commission shall, if the investment is having negative impact to the benefit of the Union and its citizens, report to the nearest Pyidaungsu Hluttaw meeting through the Union Government.

178. The Commission shall apply and follow the relevant Hluttaw Committees and Commissions as consultative bodies when the advices are required during the performing of its duties.

179. The investor is allowed the business related technologies as a contribution of investment. The said technologies are valued by the international valuation standards stipulated by the International Valuation Standards Council.

180. The Myanmar Language or Myanmar and English Languages shall be used when the documents prepared and communications made for the investment and only based on the documents written by the Myanmar Language if the differences in interpretation arise between the two languages.

Union Minister
Ministry of National Planning and Economic Development

Schedule (1)
Manufacturing and Service Businesses which can carry out by the Citizens only
(Referring to the Rule 7)

Manufacturing Business

1. Administration and maintenance of natural forest;
2. Manufacturing the traditional medicines;
3. Extraction of crude oil manually up to 1000 feet depth;
4. Small and medium scale mineral production;
5. Production and plantation of traditional herbal plants;
6. Wholesale of semi-finished products and iron ores;
7. Production of traditional food;
8. Manufacturing the religious materials and equipments;
9. Manufacturing the traditional and cultural materials and equipments;
10. Manufacturing based on the handicraft;

Services Business

1. Private Traditional Hospitals;
2. Trading of traditional herbal raw materials;
3. Research and laboratory for Traditional medicines;
4. Ambulance transportation service;
5. Establishment of health care centres for the aged;
6. Restaurant contract, cargo transportation contract, cleaning and maintenance contract on the train;
7. Agency;
8. Generating electric power below 10 mega watt;
9. Publishing and distribution of Periodicals in language of ethnic people including Myanmar language;

Schedule (2)
**Agricultural Business and Short-Term and Long-Term Plantion Business which
can be done by Citizens only
(Referring to the Rule 8)**

1. Designated agricultural business;

Schedule (3)
Livestock Breeding Business which can be done by the Citizens only (Referring to the Rule 9)

1. Designated livestock breeding business;

Schedule (4)
Fishing Business at the Myanmar's Territorial Waters which can be carried out by the Citizens only
(Referring to the Rule 10)

1. Far distance fishing of sea fish, prawn and other water creatures at the Myanmar's territorial waters;

2. Fishing at the Ponds, lakes and other close distance fishing;

DRAFT as of December 2013

[Sample of Form]

MODEL PROSPECTUS

ABC COMPANY LIMITED

(This document is made solely for discussion purposes)

To: Director General of Directorate of Investment & Company Administration, Ministry of National Planning & Economic Development, Republic of the Union of Myanmar

Date of Filing : [_____, 2014]

Company Name : ABC Company Limited
Company Registration No. : [   ]
Date of Incorporation : [   ]

Title and Name of Representative : [Chairman, Managing Director or Director]
[Name of the Representative]

Location of the Registered Office : [_____,
Republic of the Union of Myanmar]

Place to Contact : [   ]

Telephone : [   ]

Listing : [Yangon Stock Exchange or Not Applicable]

This is to certify that this prospectus shall comply with all the requirements under the Myanmar Companies Act.

TABLE OF CONTENTS

Page

PART IV. FINANCIAL INFORMATION

PART V. OTHER INFORMATION

PART I. COMPANY INFORMATION

I. Outline of the Company

1. History / Background of the Company

The Company was incorporated as a public company on [   ] under the laws of Myanmar, having its registered address at [   ], Yangon, Myanmar. The incorporation of the Company was initiated by its group company in connection with the restructuring of the group business by transferring certain assets associated with the company business lines, according to the resolutions of board of directors and shareholders' meetings.

The following information shall be provided:

1. The legal and commercial name and website address of the company
2. The date of incorporation and the length of life of the company, etc.
3. The domicile and legal form of the company, the legislation under which the company operates, its country of incorporation and the address and phone number of its registered office. (Provide the name and address of the company's agents in each of the countries in which the shares will be offered, if any.)
4. The length of time for which the business of the company or its group has been carried on and the important events in the development of the company's business, i.e. information concerning the nature and results of any material reclassification, merger or consolidation of the company or any of its significant subsidiaries; acquisitions or dispositions of material assets other than in the ordinary course of business; any material changes in the mode of conduction the business; material changes in the types of products produced or services rendered; name changes; or the nature and results of any bankruptcy, receivership or similar proceedings with respect to the company or significant subsidiaries.
5. A description of the company's material capital expenditures and divestitures, since the beginning of the company's last two financial years to the date of the

Prospectus.

6. Information concerning the material capital expenditures and divestitures currently in progress, including the distribution of these investments geographically and the method of financing.

2. Organizational Structure of the Company and its Group

Provide the company's structure by showing intra/inter-companies' trees in the diagrams. If the company is part of a group, include a brief description of the group and the company's position within the group.

3. Outline of Parent, Subsidiaries and Associated Companies

Provide information on each of the company's subsidiaries and associated companies which account for 10% or more of the absolute amount of the net assets, net liabilities or profit or loss before tax, respectively, of the group for any of the two most recent financial years, including its name, country of incorporation or residence, principal place of business, principal activities and proportion of ownership interest.

4. Conditions of Employees

Disclose the information on the latest company's employees, such as number of employees, categories of employees and age of employees, etc.

As at the end of the latest financial year, there were [   ] employees consisting of:
- Full time employees: [   ]
- Part time employees: [   ]
- Contract employees: [   ]

Provide the table of the professional qualification and age of the employees as at the latest account closing date, if applicable.

II. Description of Business

1. Nature of Business

The information required by this section may be presented on the same basis as that used to determine the company's business segments under the body of accounting principles used in preparing the financial statements. The following information shall be provided:

- A description of the nature of the company's operations and its principal activities, stating the main categories of products sold and/or services performed for each of the last two financial years. Indicate any significant new products and/or services that have been introduced between the beginning of the period comprising the two most recent completed financial years and the latest practicable date and, to the extent the development of new products or services has been publicly disclosed, give the status of development.
- A description f the seasonality of the company's main business.
- A description of the sources and availability of raw materials, including a description of whether prices of principal raw materials are volatile.
- Summary information regarding the extent to which the company is dependent, if at all, on patents or licenses, industrial, commercial or financial contracts (including contracts with customers or suppliers) or new manufacturing processes, where such factors are material to the company's business or profitability.
- A description of the material effects of government regulations on the company's business, identifying the regulatory body.

2. Outline of Each Business Segment
Provide the segment information for each of the business lines with respect to the products, services, activities, locations by sector, division or department.

3. Sales and Marketing
State a description of the marketing channels used by the company, including an explanation of any special sales methods, such as installment sales.

4. Competition
Provide a description of the principal markets in which the company competes, including a breakdown of total revenues by category of activity and geographic market for each of the last two financial years.
Also describe the basis for any statements made by the company regarding its

competitive position shall be disclosed.

5. Material Contracts

Provide a summary of each material contract, other than contracts entered into in the ordinary course of business, to which the company or any member of the group is a party, for the two years immediately preceding the date of the Prospectus, including dates, parties, general nature of the contracts, terms and conditions, and amount of any consideration passing to or from the company or any other member of the group.

6. Property, Plant and Equipment

Provide information regarding any material tangible fixed assets, including leased properties, and any major encumbrances thereon, including a description of the size and uses of the property; productive capacity and extent of utilization of the company's facilities for each of the last two financial years; how the assets are held; the products produced; and the location.

Describe any regulatory requirements and environmental issues that may materially affect the company's utilization of the assets. With regard to any material plans to construct, expand or improve facilities, describe the nature of and reason for the plan, an estimate of the amount of expenditures including the amount of expenditures already paid, a description of the method of financing the activity, the estimated dates of start and completion of the activity, and the increase of production capacity anticipated after completion.

7. Research and Development

Provide a description of the company's research and development policies for the last two financial years, where it is significant, including the amount spent during each of the last two financial years on company-sponsored research and development activities.

8. Other Related Business

Describe any relevant information on other business lines relating to environmental and social impact issues, if applicable.

PART II. INFORMATION ON THE COMPANY'S MANAGEMENT AND SHAREHOLDERS

Ⅰ. Board of Directors and Directors

The following table sets out the short biography of directors specifying their identity and qualifications.

Name	Title	Representativ e of Institution	Gender	Nationality	Date/Place of Birth	Education

Other than specified in the company act, the board of directors of the company has responsibility for the administrative affairs of the company and has specific responsibilities as follows:

- to consider the company's strategy, as well as implementation plan of the company;
- to consider and determine the remunerations and compensation of the chief executive officer and top management;
- to consider and determine the capital, its usage, its structure, the ratio of the capital and loan, as well as loan agreements, credit facility agreements, joint venture agreements, electricity sale and purchase agreement and other agreements with high value;
- to propose an external auditor;
- to consider the appointment or removal of an agent to be in the board of directors of the joint venture company, if any;
- to adopt the appointment or removal of the accounting department manager

and the manager of internal audit's office as proposed by the chief executive officer; and

- to propose the remunerations of the external auditor.

[The board of directors dose not involve in the day-to-day operations of the company unless any of the directors is appointed as the management.]

II. Senior Management

The senior management is appointed by the board of directors. In the appointment of each position of the management team, the qualifications of the candidates are considered whether they are suitable to each position.

The following table sets forth the short bio of the senior management of the company.

Name	Title	Gender	Nationality	Date/Place of Birth	Education

III. Remuneration / Compensation of Senior Management

The following table sets out the remuneration or compensation of the management.

Name	Position	Aggregate Amount (Salary and Compensation) (thousand in Kyat)	
		2013	2014

IV. Corporate Governance

The following committees have been established under the board of directors: an audit committee, a nomination and remuneration committee, a strategy and investment committee and a risk management committee. Each of the committees operates in accordance with terms and standards established by the board of directors.

- Audit Committee

The company has established an audit committee with the terms and standards in compliance with the corporate governance code of the listing rules. The primary duties of the audit committee include, but are not limited to, the following:

(i) review the company's material financial and accounting policies and practices and their implementation, supervise its financial operation status;

(ii) evaluate audit controller's performance and make recommendations to the board;

(iii) review the company's fundamental internal audit system and make recommendations to the board, approve the annual audit plan and budget, direct the internal audit process and monitor its effectiveness;

(iv) review annually the soundness and effectiveness of its internal control system, promptly consider and process any major complaints;

(v) coordinate between the internal and external auditor, supervise the improvement and implementation of any significant findings arising out of the internal and external audit;

(vi) make recommendations to the board on the appointment, removal, and remuneration of the external auditor, supervise the external auditor's independence and objectivity, and the effectiveness of the audit process in accordance with applicable standards;

(vii) ensure that the board will provide a timely response to the issues raised in the external auditor's management letter;

(viii) review the annual audit report prepared by the external auditor and other professional recommendations;

(ix) perform an initial assessment on any related transactions that are to be approved at a shareholders' meeting and board meeting and submit it to the board for approval;

(x) review and approve or accept filings of related transaction as authorized by the board; and

(xi) perform other duties as required by applicable laws, regulations, or other matters authorized by the board.

- Nomination and Remuneration Committee

The company has established an audit committee with the terms and standards in compliance with the corporate governance code of the listing rules. The primary duties of the nomination and remuneration committee include, but are not limited to, the following:

(i) study the selection standards and procedures for the directors and senior management hired by the board, review at least annually the structure, size and composition of the board and make recommendations on any proposed changes to the board to complement the corporate strategy;

(ii) broadly search for qualified individuals as candidates suitably to become the director and senior management;

(iii) review and approve the remuneration proposals of directors and senior management hired by the board with reference to the board's corporate goals and objectives; and

(iv) make independent and prudent suggestions relating to the dismissal or removal of directors.

- Strategy and Investment Committee

The company has established an audit committee with the terms and standards in compliance with the corporate governance code of the listing rules. The primary duties of the strategy and investment committee include, but are not limited to, the following:

(i) review and make proposals on the general development strategy and specific strategic development plans, and make recommendations to the board;

(ii) evaluate factors that may have an impact on the strategic development plans and its implementation in light of domestic and international economic financial conditions and market changes and make prompt strategic adjustment recommendations to the board;

(iii) review the annual financial budget and final accounts plans, and make recommendations to the board;

(iv) review the external investment proposals and explain them at shareholders' and board meetings upon their request;

(v) develop and revise policies related to the corporate governance, and make recommendations to the board;

(vi) supervise the directors and senior management's training and continuing professional development;

(vii) develop, amend and supervise the internal code of conduct for the directors and employees; and

(viii) supervise the disclosure on corporate governance in compliance with the relevant rules and regulations of the stock exchange on which the company's shares are listed.

- Risk Management Committee

The company has established an audit committee with the terms and standards in compliance with the corporate governance code of the listing rules. The primary duties of the risk management committee include, but are not limited to, the following:

(i) be responsible for the risk management, be completely familiar with the significant risks and the corresponding management status, supervise the operational effectiveness of the risk management controls;

(ii) review the overall goals, fundamental policies and procedures for risk management, and make suggestions and recommendations to the board;

(iii) review and approve the risk management organization and corresponding responsibilities, and make suggestions and recommendations to the board;

(iv) review the annual risk assessment report and make suggestions and recommendations to the board;

(v) review and submit the annual compliance report to the board; and

(vi) develop and amend the internal compliance code applicable to the employees and directors, assess and supervise the compliance policies and status, and make recommendations to the board.

V. Shareholders

The following table sets out the general information on the major shareholders of the company [as of the data of this Prospectus].

Name	Address	Quantity	Percentage of Ownership

3. 외국인 투자허가(MIC PERMIT) 신청서 **167**

VI. Dividends, Dividend Policy and Stock Options

1. Dividend Policy

The Company will pay dividends, if any, only out of its profits, and subject to its cash flow, as permitted under the Myanmar law. The expected dividend payout ratio is [50]% of the Company's net profit before tax for the respective financial years. Dividends will be paid in Myanmar Kyat.

The board of directors of the Company has the discretion to recommend the payment of dividends. The Company cannot assure the investors that the Company will declare or pay out any dividends.

2. Stock Options

The company has not granted any stock options to its directors and employees.

VII. Description of the Company's Shares

Set out here is certain general information relating to the shares of the company, including brief summaries of certain provision of its contract of incorporation and the articles of association, the company act and the relevant rules/regulations, all as currently in effect.

PART III. RELATED PARTY TRANSACTIONS

Provide the information required below for the period since the beginning of the company's preceding two/three financial years up to the date of the Prospectus, with respect to transactions or loans between the company and its related parties.

Describe the nature and extent of any transactions or presently proposed transactions which are material to the company or the related party, or any transactions that are unusual in their nature or conditions, involving goods, services, or tangible or intangible assets, to which the company or any of its parent or subsidiaries was a party.

I. Material Transactions / Agreements with Major Shareholders

Disclose the transactions with shareholders holding at least 5% of the outstanding shares, indicating name, type and date of transactions, during the last two/three years prior to the filing of application.

II. Material Transactions / Agreements with Senior Management

Provide the material transactions with directors or senior officers or persons whereby directors or senior officers of the company has interest during the last two/three years prior to the filing of application.

Also disclose material transactions with family members of directors or senior officers or shareholders holding at least 5% of the outstanding shares during the last two/three years.

Further present material transactions with persons who have relationship with directors of the company, its subsidiary or holding company where relationship occurred in the transaction or any arrangement with the company during the last two/three years.

Describe the material transactions with directors receiving any interest or professional fee for services in which the director provided via any firm to the company during the last two/three years.

III. Other Conflicts of Interests

Where a director or significant person of the company or associates has an interest in any entity carrying on the same business or dealing in similar products as the company or the group, disclose:

- Name of the entity;
- Name of the director or significant person involved;
- Nature and extent of his/her interest in that entity and the extent to which he/she is involved in the management of that entity either directly or indirectly; or
- Whether any conflict of interests thereby arising has been or is to be resolved or mitigated and, if so, how it has been or is proposed to be resolved or mitigated.

If any of the named experts, counselors, underwriter or other financial adviser was employed on a contingent basis, owns an amount of shares in the company or its subsidiaries which is material to that person, has a material, direct or indirect economic interest in the company or that depends on the success of the offering, or otherwise has a material relationship with the company, provide a brief description of the nature and terms of such contingency, interest or relationship.

PART Ⅳ. FINANCIAL INFORMATION

Ⅰ. Financial Statements with Notes

Attach the audited financial statements.

1. The Prospectus must contain comparative consolidated financial statements of the company, or if the company is a holding company, of the group, that cover the latest two financial years (or such shorter period that the company has been in operation).

2. If the registration/effective date of the Prospectus is more than six months after the end of the most recent completed financial year for which financial statements is provided above, the Prospectus must contain interim financial statements of the company, or if the company is a holding company, of the group, made up to a date that is not earlier than six months before the registration/effective date of the Prospectus. The Prospectus must also include comparative interim financial statements (other than a statement of financial position) for the corresponding period in the previous financial year.

3. The financial statements to be provided under paragraph 1 and 2 of this section must be:
   - prepared in accordance with the Myanmar Financial Reporting Standards and/or any other accounting principles accepted in Myanmar; and
   - other than the comparative interim financial statements, if any, which need not be audited, the financial statements are to be audited in accordance with the Myanmar Auditing Standards and/or any other accounting principles accepted in Myanmar.

4. The financial statements to be provided under paragraph 1 and 2 of this section shall comprise such items as required by the accounting principles.

II. Auditor's Report

Describe or attach here the whole auditor's report on the company's financial statements.

III. Legal Proceedings / Litigations

Provide information on any legal or arbitration proceedings, including those relating to bankruptcy, receivership or similar proceedings which may have, or have had in the 12 months immediately preceding the date of the Prospectus, significant effects on the company's financial position or profitability. This includes governmental proceedings pending or known to be contemplated.

PART V. OTHER INFORMATION

I. Signature of Chairman, Managing Director and Director

Provide the signatures of chairman, managing director and/or director of the company certifying that the entire information contained herein the Prospectus is accurate and complete.

II. Status of Directors, Senior Management, Corporate Secretary, Auditors and Advisors

Provide the identification, sign-offs, consents or statements, if applicable, of the company's management and the relevant experts, including, but not limited to, independent auditor, legal adviser, tax adviser and consultants, contributing to the preparation of this Prospectus.

III. Others

Provide any other relevant matters in relation to the execution or documentation of the share offering, such as the certain provisions of the Company's memorandum and articles of association under the Myanmar Companies Act. Otherwise, simply put "not applicable" in here.

Form (1)

Proposal Form of Investor/Promoter for the investment to be made in the Republic of the Union of Myanmar

To,

    Chairman

    Myanmar Investment Commission

Reference No.

Date.

I do apply for the permission to make investment in the Republic of the Union of Myanmar in accordance with the Foreign Investment Law by furnishing the following particulars:

1. The Investor's or Promoter's:
   - (a) Name ....
   - (b) Father's name ....
   - (c) ID No./National Registration Card No./Passport No. ....
   - (d) Citizenship ....
   - (e) Address: ....
     - (i) Address in Myanmar ....
     - (ii) Residence abroad ....
   - (f) Name of principle organization ....
   - (g) Type of business ....
   - (h) Principle company's address: ....
     ....

2. If the investment business is formed under Joint Venture, partners':
   - (a) Name ....
   - (b) Father's name ....
   - (c) ID No./ National Registration Card No./Passport No. ....

(d) Citizenship ....

(e) Address: ....

　(i) Address in Myanmar ....

　(ii) Residence abroad ....

(f) Parent company ....

(g) Type of business ....

(h) Parent company's address: ....

....

Remark: The following documents need to attach according to the above
paragraph (1) and (2):

　(1) Company registration certificate (copy);

　(2) National Registration Card (copy) and passport (copy);

　(3) Evidences about the business and financial conditions of the
participants of the proposed investment business;

3. Type of proposed investment business:

(a) Manufacturing ....

(b) Service business related with manufacturing ....

....

(c) Service ....

(d) Others ....

Remark: Expressions about the nature of business with regard to the above
paragraph (3)

4. Type of business organization to be formed:

(a) One hundred percent ....

(b) Joint Venture: ....

　(i) Foreigner and citizen ....

　(ii) Foreigner and Government department/organization ....

....

(c) By contractual basis:

　(i) Foreigner and citizen ....

(ii) Foreigner and Government department/organization ....
....

Remark: The following information needs to attach for the above Paragraph (4):
  (i) Share ratio for the authorized capital from abroad and local, names,
  citizenships, addresses and occupations of the directors;
  (ii) Joint Venture Agreement (Draft) and recommendation of the Union
  Attorney General Office if the investment is related with the State;
  (iii) Contract (Agreement) (Draft)

5. Particulars relating to company incorporation
  (a) Authorized capital ....
  (b) Type of share ....
  (c) Number of shares ....
  ....

Remark: Memorandum of Association and Articles of Association of the Company
  shall be submitted with regard to above paragraph 5.

6. Particulars relating to capital of the investment business

Kyat/US$ (Million)

  (a) Amount/percentage of local capital
  to be contributed   ....
  (b) Amount/percentage of foreign capital
  to be brought in   ....
  _____

                              Total   _____

  (c) Annually or period of proposed capital to be brought in
  ....
  (d) Last date of capital brought in
  ....
  (e) Proposed duration of investment ....

(f) Commencement date of construction ....

(g) Construction period ....

Remark: Describe with annexure if it is required for the above Para 6 (c).

7. Detail list of foreign capital to be brought in

	Foreign Currency (Million)	Equivalent Kyat (Million)
(a) Foreign currency (Type and amount)	....	....
(b) Machinery and equipment and value (to enclose detail list)	....	....
(c) List of initial raw materials and value (to enclose detail list)	....	....
(d) Value of licence, intellectual property, industrial design, trade mark, patent rights, etc.	....	....
(e) Value of technical know-how	....	....
(f) Others	....	....
Total	_____	_____

Remark: The evidence of permission shall be submitted for the above para 7 (d) and (e).

8. Details of local capital to be contributed

	Kyat (Million)
(a) Amount	....
(b) Value of machinery and equipment (to enclose detail list)	....
(c) Rental rate for building/land	....
(d) Cost of building construction	....
(e) Value of furniture and assets (to enclose detail list)	....

(f) Value of initial raw material requirement   ....

    (to enclose detail list)

(g) Others   ....

                                            Total   _____

9. Particulars about the investment business -

   (a) Investment location(s)/place ....

   ....

   (b) Type and area requirement for land or land and building ....

      (i) Location ....

      (ii) Number of land/building and area ....

      (iii) Owner of the land ....

          (aa) Name/company/department ....

          (bb) National Registration Card No. ....

          (cc) Address ....

          ....

      (iv) Type of land ....

      (v) Period of land lease contract ....

      (vi) Lease period .... From .... To (   ) year

      (vii) Lease rate ....

          (aa) Land ....

          (bb) Building ....

      (viii) Ward ....

      (ix) Township ....

      (x) State/Region ....

      (xi) Lessee ....

          (aa) Name/ Name of Company/Department ....

          (bb) Father's name ....

          (cc) Citizenship ....

          (dd) ID No./Passport No. ....

          (ee) Residence Address ....

Remark: Following particulars have to enclosed for above Para 9 (b)

      (i) to enclose land map, land ownership and ownership evidences;

(ii) draft land lease agreement, recommendation from the Union Attorney General Office if the land is related to the State;

(c) Requirement of building to be constructed;

    (i) Type / number of building ....

    (ii) Area ....

(d) Product to be produced/ Service ....

    (1) Name of product ....

    (2) Estimate amount to be produced annually ....

    (3) Type of service ....

    (4) Estimate value of service annually ....

Remark: Detail list shall be enclosed with regard to the above para 9 (d).

(e) Annual requirement of materials/ raw materials

Remark: According to the above para 9 (e) detail list of products in terms of type of products, quantity, value, technical specifications for the production shall be listed and enclosed.

(f) Production system ....

(g) Technology ....

(h) System of sales ....

(i) Annual fuel requirement ....

    (to prescribe type and quantity)

(j) Annual electricity requirement ....

(k) Annual water requirement ....

    (to prescribe daily requirement, if any)

10. Detail information about financial standing

(a) Name/company's name ....

(b) ID No./National Registration Card No./Passport No. ....

(c) Bank Account No. ....

Remark: To enclose bank statement from resident country or annual audit report of the principle company with regard to the above para 10.

11. Number of personnel required for the proposed economic activity:

(a) Local personnel   (   ) number   (   ) %

(b) Foreign experts and technicians   (   ) number   (   ) %

(Engineer, QC, Buyer, Management, etc. based on the nature of business and required period)

Remark: As per para 11 the following information shall be enclosed:

    (i) Number of personnel, occupation, salary, etc;

    (ii) Social security and welfare arrangements for personnel;

    (iii) family accompany with foreign employee;

12. Particulars relating to economic justification:

	Foreign Currency	Equivalent Estimated Kyat
(a) Annual income	....	....
(b) Annual expenditure	....	....
(c) Annual net profit	....	....
(d) Yearly investments	....	....
(e) Recoupment period	....	....
(f) Other benefits	....	....

    (to enclose detail calculations)

13. Evaluation of environmental impact:

    (a) Organization for evaluation of environmental assessment;

    (b) Duration of the evaluation for environmental assessment;

    (c) Compensation programme for environmental damages

    (d) Water purification system and waste water treatment system;

    (e) Waste management system;

    (f) System for storage of chemicals

14. Evaluation on social impact assessments:

    (a) Organization for evaluation of social impact assessments;

    (b) Duration of the evaluation for social impact assessments;

    (c) Corporate social responsibility programme;

Signature   ....

Name   ....

Designation   ....

Form (2)

The Republic of the Union of Myanmar Myanmar Investment Commission Permit

Permit No. ....   Date ....

This Permit is issued by the Myanmar Investment Commission according to the section 13, sub-section (b) of the Republic of the Union of Myanmar Foreign Investment Law:

(a) Name of Investor/Promoter ....

(b) Citizenship ....

(c) Residence address ....

....

(d) Name and address of Principle Organization ....

....

(e) Place of Incorporation ....

(f) Type of business in which investment is to be made ....

(g) Place(s) at which investment is permitted ....

....

(h) Amount of foreign capital ....

(i) Period for bringing in foreign capital ....

(j) Total amount of capital (Kyat) ....

....

(k) Construction period ....

(l) Validity of investment permit ....

(m) Form of investment ....

(n) Name of company incorporated in Myanmar ....

Chairman
Myanmar Investment Commission

Form (3)

To,

Chairman
Myanmar Investment Commission
The Republic of the Union of Myanmar

Reference. No.

Date.

Subject: Submission of Quarterly Performance Report

1. I do submit the Quarterly Performance Report which is approved by the Permit of Myanmar Investment Commission (MIC) according to the Foreign Investment Rules.

2. The particulars about the business permitted by Myanmar Investment Commission (MIC) are as follow:
   (a) Name of Investor / Promoter ....
   (b) Myanmar Investment Commission (MIC) Permit No ....

3. Hereby submitted within three months period from, ... (month)............ (year) to .... (month) .... (year), of ....
.... Company enclosed herewith the required documents.

Signature   ....
Name   ....
Designation   ....

Form (4)

To,

    Chairman

    Myanmar Investment Commission

    The Republic of the Union of Myanmar

Reference No.

Date.

Subject: Sub-leasing of permitted land and building

I, hereby submitted the application with the following particulars for the sub leasing of permitted land and building to be used under section 17, sub-section (e) of the Foreign Investment Law:

1. Particulars about the original owner of land and building:

    (a) Name of owner/organization ....

    (b) Area ....

    (c) Location ....

    (d) Original period permitted to use the land (validity of land grant) ....

    (e) Payment of long term lease as capital   Yes (   )   No (   )

    (f) Agreed by original lessor   Yes (   )   No (   )

2. Lessor

    (a) Name of investor/promoter ....

    (b) Myanmar Investment Commission Permit No. ....

3. Lessee

    (a) Name ....

    (b) ID No./National Registration Card No./Passport No. ....

    (c) Citizenship ....

    (d) Company's Name ....

    ....

(e) Address ....
....

4. Particulars relating to land and building in which investment is permitted by Myanmar Investment Commission:
    (a) Type of investment ....
    (b) Investment location (s) ....
    ....
    (c) Area ....
    (d) Size and number of building(s) ....
    (e) Value of land/building ....

5. Original validity period permitted by Commission: ....

6. Period for sub-leasing ....

7. Important particulars from the original Land and Building Leasing Agreement signed by both parties:
    (a) Lessor ....
    (b) Lessee ....
    (c) Area ....
    (d) Location ....
    ....
    (e) Lease Period ....

8. Submission of sub-lease agreement (Draft)
(to enclose recommendation letter from the Union Attorney General Office for Government organization)

Applicant

Investor / Promoter

Form (5)

To,

Chairman

Myanmar Investment Commission

The Republic of the Union of Myanmar

Reference No.

Date.

Subject: Mortgage of land and building permitted for investment

I, hereby submitted the application with the following particulars for mortgage the land and building to be used for the business permitted under section 17, sub-section(e) of the Foreign Investment Law:

1. Particulars about the original owner of land and building:
   (a) Name of owner/organization ....
   (b) Area ....
   (c) Location ....
   (d) Original period permitted to use the land (Validity of land grant) ....
   (e) Payment of long term lease as capital   Yes (   )   No (   )
   (f) Agreed by original Lessor   Yes (   )   No (   )

2. Mortgagor
   (a) Name of investor/promoter ....
   (b) Myanmar Investment Commission Permit No. ....

3. Mortgagee
   (a) Name ....
   (b) ID No./National Registration Card No./Passport No. ....
   (c) Citizenship ....
   (d) Company's Name ....
   (e) Address ....

4. Particulars relating to land and building in which investment is permitted by Myanmar Investment Commission:

    (a) Type of investment ....

    (b) Investment location (s) ....

    ....

    (c) Area ....

    (d) Size and number of building (s) ....

    (e) Value of land/building ....

5. Original validity period permitted by Commission: ....

6. Period of Mortgage ....

7. Important particulars from the original Land and Building Lease Agreement signed by both parties:

    (a) Lessor ....

    (b) Lessee ....

    (c) Land area ....

    (d) Location ....

    ....

    (e) Lease period ....

8. Submission of Mortgagee Agreement (Draft)

(to enclose recommendation letter from the Union Attorney General Office for Government organization)

Applicant

Investor / Promoter

Form (6)

To,

Chairman

Myanmar Investment Commission

The Republic of the Union of Myanmar

Reference No.

Date.

Subject: Transfer of all shares

I do hereby submit the following information and applied for the transfer of all shares in accordance with the section 17, sub-section (i) of the Foreign Investment Law:

1. Transferor

    (a) Name of Investor/Promoter ....

    (b) Company Name /Type of business ....

    (c) Company Registration No. ....

2. Transferee

    (a) Name ....

    (b) Company Name / Type of business ....

    (c) Company Registration No. ....

    (d) ID No./National Registration Card No./Passport No. ....

    (e) Citizenship ....

    (f) Designation/Responsibilities ....

    (g) Residence Address/Company Address ....

3. Information relating to the transfer of shares

    (a) Total number of shares ....

    (b) Par value ....

    (c) Number of shares to be transferred ....

4. Validity of investment permitted by Commission ....

5. Submitted with the share transfer form   Yes (   )

                                                    No (   )

6. Resolution of Board of Director (BOD) of the Company permitted by the Commission

    Yes (   )

    No (   )

                                                            Applicant

                                                    Investor / Promoter

Form (7)

To,

    Chairman

    Myanmar Investment Commission

    The Republic of the Union of Myanmar

Reference No.

Date.

Subject: Transfer of part of shares

I hereby submitted the following information and applied for the transfer of part of shares in accordance with the section 17, sub-section (j) of the Foreign Investment Law:

1. Transferor

    (a) Name of Investor / Promoter ....

    (b) Company Name / Type of business ....

    (c) Company Registration No. ....

2. Transferee

    (a) Name ....

    (b) Company Name / Type of business ....

    (c) Company Registration No. ....

    (d) ID No./National Registration Card No./Passport No. ....

    (e) Citizenship ....

    (f) Designation/Responsibilities ....

    (g) Residence Address/Company Address ....

        ....

3. Information relating to the transferred shares

    (a) Total number of shares ....

    (b) Par value ....

    (c) Number of shares to be transferred ....

4. Validity investment period permitted by Commission ....

5. Submitted with the share transfer form   Yes (   )

                                                        No (   )

6. Resolution of Board of Director (BOD) of the Company permitted by the Commission

    Yes (   )

    No (   )

                                                          Applicant

                                             Investor / Promoter

Form (8)

To,

Chairman

Myanmar Investment Commission

The Republic of the Union of Myanmar

Reference No.

Date.

Subject: Application of work permit for the foreign employees to appoint at the investment business permitted by the Myanmar Investment Commission

I do hereby submit the following information and apply for the work permit for the foreign employee who is working at the investment business permitted under the Foreign Investment Law in accordance with the section 25 of the Foreign Investment Law:

1. Applicant

   (a) Name of Investor/Promoter ....

   (b) Myanmar Investment Commission Permit No. ....

2. Particulars relating to the applicant

   (a) Name ....

   (b) ID No./Passport No. ....

   (c) Citizenship ....

   (d) Residence Address ....

   (e) Number of proposed employee in the original proposal ....

   (f) Number of already appointed employees ....

3. Recommended by Directorate of Labour   Yes (   )

                                               No (   )

Applicant

Investor / Promoter

Form (9)

To,

    Chairman

    Myanmar Investment Commission

    The Republic of the Union of Myanmar

                    Reference No.

                    Date.

Subject: Application of stay permit for the foreign employees to appoint at the investment business permitted by the Myanmar Investment Commission

I do hereby submit the following information and applied for the stay permit for the foreign employee who is working at the investment business permitted under the Foreign Investment Law in accordance with the section 25 of the Foreign Investment Law:

1. Applicant

    (a) Name of Investor/Promoter ....

    (b) Myanmar Investment Commission Permit No. ....

2. Particulars relating to the applicant

    (a) Name ....

    (b) ID No./ Passport No. ....

    (c) Citizenship ....

    (d) Residence Address ....

        ....

3. Particulars relating to the dependent(s) to the applicant

    (a) Name ....

    (b) ID No./Passport No. ....

    (c) Citizenship ....

    (d) Residence Address ....

        ....

4. Number of proposed employees in the original proposal

5. Number of appointed employees

6. Recommended by Department of Immigration and National Registration
   Yes (   )
   No (   )

Applicant

Investor / Promoter

Form (10)

To,

Chairman

Myanmar Investment Commission

The Republic of the Union of Myanmar

Reference No.

Date.

Subject: Application of exemption and reliefs in accordance with the Foreign Investment Law

I do hereby as an investor/ promoter, apply the exemptions and reliefs stipulated in the Chapter XII, section 27 (b) to (k) of the Foreign Investment Law according to Foreign Investment Rules:

1. Applicant

   (a) Name of Investor/Promoter ....

   (b) Myanmar Investment Commission Permit No. ....

2. Construction period/ renovation period as per original proposal

3. Commencement of commercial operation date

4. Applied for the following exemptions and reliefs as per Chapter XII, section 27 (b) to (k) of the Foreign Investment Law:

   (a) Exemption/relief as per Chapter XII, section 27 (b) of the Foreign Investment Law

   (b) Exemption/relief as per Chapter XII, section 27 (c) of the Foreign Investment Law

   ( )

   ( )

   ( )

   (j) Exemption/relief as per Chapter XII, section 27 (k) of the Foreign Investment Law

Applicant

Investor / Promoter

Form (11)

To,

Chairman

Myanmar Investment Commission

The Republic of the Union of Myanmar

Reference No.

Date.

Subject: Report for the commencement of the commercial operation date for the manufacturing or service

I do hereby inform the commencement of the commercial operation date for the manufacturing (or) service business in accordance with the Foreign Investment Rules para 98:

1. Applicant ....

    (a) Name of Investor/Promoter ....

    (b) Myanmar Investment Commission Permit No. ....

2. Construction period/renovation period as per original proposal ....

3. Date of sales of product/service ....

4. Type of product / service ....

5. Volume of product / service ....

6. Value of product / service ....

7. Export licence No. and date ....

8. Type of product to be exported ....

9. Export Quantity ....

10. Value of Export ....

11. Commercial operation date ....

Applicant

Investor / Promoter

Form (12)

To,

Chairman

Myanmar Investment Commission

The Republic of the Union of Myanmar

Reference No.

Date.

Subject: Application for permit to lease the land for the investment business

I do hereby apply with the following information for permit to lease the land or permit to use the land according to the Foreign Investment Rules:

1. Particulars relating to original owner of land and building

    (a) Name of owner/organization ....

    (b) Area ....

    (c) Location ....

    (d) Original period permitted to use the land (Validity of land grant) ....

    (e) Payment of long term lease as equity   Yes (   )   No (   )

    (f) Agreed by original Lessor   Yes (   )   No (   )

2. Lessor

    (a) Name / company's name/ department/ organization ....

    (b) National Registration Card No/ Passport No. ....

    (c) Address ....

    ....

3. Lessee

    (a) Name/ company's name /department/ organization ....

    (b) ID No./National Registration Card No./Passport No. ....

    (c) Citizenship ....

    (d) Address ....

    ....

4. Particulars relating to the proposed lease land
   (a) Type of investment ....
   (b) Investment location(s) ....
   ....
   (c) Area ....
   (d) Size and number of building (s) ....
   (e) Value of building ....

5. Submission of Land Lease Agreement (Draft)
(to enclose recommendation letter from the Union Attorney General Office for Government organization)

6. Land lease rate (per square meter per year)

7. Land use premium – LUP) (If the land is belonged to government organization the LUP shall pay in cash by the lessee.)
Rate/ per acre: ....

8. Agreed by original land lessor or land user
   Yes (   )
   No (   )

9. Lease Period

                                                          Applicant

                                    Investor / Promoter

Form (13)

To,

Chairman

Myanmar Investment Commission

The Republic of the Union of Myanmar

Reference. No.

Date.

Subject: Application for the permit of foreign currency repatriation

Referring to the Foreign Exchange Management Law, I do hereby apply for the repatriation of my legal income earned from the investment business as per section 40 of the Foreign Investment Law: -

1. Applicant

   (a) Name of Investor/Promoter ....

   (b) Myanmar Investment Commission Permit No. ....

2. Particulars relating to foreign currency repatriation:

   (a) Particulars of applicant: ....

       (i) Name ....

       (ii) Designation ....

       (iii) ID No./National Registration Card No./Passport No. ....

       (iv) Citizenship ....

       (v) Address ....

   (b) Type of foreign currency mentioned in original proposal ....

   (c) Source of income for the repatriation ....

       (Transfer of share/profit share/salary/dividend, etc.)

   (d) Amount to be repatriated ....

   (e) Country of beneficiary/Name of bank ....

   (f) Name of transfer bank and bank account no. ....

3. The following information are submitted correctly:

(a) Bank balance of the company

(b) Resolution of Company's Board of Director (BOD) meeting   Yes (   )

                                                                                             No (   )

(c) Share ratio (%)

(d) Commercial operation date:

(e) Operation period of the business

(f) Foreign currency repatriation period/ frequency

Applicant

Investor / Promoter

부록 4

To:

The Director General

Directorate of Investment and Company Administration

The Government of the Republic of the Union of Myanmar

No. 1, Thitsar Road, Yankin Township, Yangon

Date: ....

Re: Application to check availability of company name for foreign company registration

1. I wish to submit an application to confirm the availability of the following company name:

Name in English: ....

Name in Myanmar: ....

(The proposed company name must be specified in both English & Myanmar).

2. The contact details of the applicant are as listed below:

Name: ....

Company: ....

Address: ....

....

Phone number: ....

3. The business objectives and activities of the proposed foreign company are as listed below:

(i) ....

(ii) ....

(iii) ....

(iv) ....

(v) ....

(vi) ....

(vii) ....

(viii) ....

Signature of applicant: ....

Name: ....

NRC (Myanmar) or Passport No. (and country): ....

To:

The Director General

Directorate of Investment and Company Administration The Government of the Republic of the Union of Myanmar No. 1, Thitsar Road, Yankin Township, Yangon

Date: ....

Dear Sir,

I hereby submit the following documents for registration and application for Permit, which are required under the Myanmar Companies Act 1914.

Should you need further information regarding these documents, I am pleased to furnish them without any hesitation.

1. Declaration of registration (Form 1)
2. Situation of registered office form
3. Declaration of Legal Version
4. Certificate of Translation
5. Statement of company objectives & Undertaking not to conduct trading
6. Directors details (Form 26)
7. Memorandum of Association (2 copies)
8. Articles of Association (2 copies)
9. Application Form for Permit (Form A)
10. Copy of passport of shareholder or copy of directors' resolution
11. Copy of passport of foreign directors or copy of N.R.C for local directors

Yours sincerely,

....

Signature of proposed director

Name: ....

FORM A

APPLICATION FOR PERMIT TO TRADE

(See Regulation 3)

Note: This application is to be accompanied by;

1. A copy of the Company's Memorandum and Articles of Association or of the chapter, Statutes of other instruments constituting or defining the constitution of the Company.

2. Copies of the Company's Balance Sheet and Profit and loss Accounts for the last two years preceding the application.

Application by a Foreign Company or Company carrying on International Trade for issue of a Permit under Section 27 A of the Myanmar Companies Act:

(1)		Name of Company	
(2)		Country of incorporation of Company	
(3)	(a)	Names, addresses and nationality of shareholders in case of companies incorporated in the Republic of the Union of Myanmar	
	(b)	Number of citizens or non-citizen shareholders together with the number of shares held by them separated in the case of companies incorporated outside the Republic of the Union of Myanmar	
(4)	(a)	Location of Company's Head Office	
	(b)	The location of Company's principal office in the Republic of the Union of Myanmar	
(5)		The objects for which the Company is formed (field of business)	
(6)	(a)	The amount of capital and the number of shares into which the capital is divided	
	(b)	If more than one class of share is authorized, the decription of each class and the rights and privileges pertaining to each	
	(c)	Amount of capital brought or to be brought into the Republic of the Union of Myanmar	

	(d)	Whether there is any discrimination among different classes of shareholders with regard to number of votes he may cast	
(7)	(a)	The maximum amount of indebtedness if any which may be incurred by the company and	
	(b)	The prohibition against the contracting of debts in excess of that amount	
(8)		Period for which Permit is applied for	
(9)		The offices who are to conduct the affairs of the company, dutes of each, and the authority of the Board of Directors to fill the positions above named	
(10)		The number of Directors, the manner of their appointments and their powers	
(11)		The names, addresses and nationality of the Directors for the current year	
(12)		The names, addresses and nationality of the promoters	
(13)		Statements in compliance with legal require-ments for initial capital including the amount to be paid in before commencement of business	

(Director)

FORM 1

DECLARATION OF REGISTRATION OF COMPANY

MYANMAR COMPANY ACT

(See Section 24)

Declaration in compliance with the requirements of the Myanmar Companies Act, 1913 made pursuant to Section 24(2) on behalf of a Company proposed to be registered as;

Presented for filing by ;

I,

do solemnly and sincerely declare that all the requirements of the Myanmar Companies Act, 1913 in respect of matters precedent to the registration of the said Company and incidental thereto have been complied with save only the payment of fees and sums payable on registration and I make this solemn declaration conscientiously believing the same to be true.

SIGNATURE ....

WITNESS (DIRECTOR)

for and on behalf of
the Board of Directors

Nay Pyi Taw

the　　　　　　day of

CERTIFICATE OF TRANSLATION

I, the undersigned, do hereby certify that the work of translation from the original Memorandum & Articles of Association in English of " " into Myanmar was done by me , and the translation is correct to the best of my knowledge.

Nay Pyi   Taw

Dated, the   day of

NOTICE OF THE SITUATION OF THE REGISTERED OFFICE
OF THE

To

Director General
Directorate of Investment and Company Administration Department
Ministry of National Planning and Economic Development
Office (32),Nay Pyi Taw.

The abovenamed Company hereby give you notice, in accordance with the provisions of the Myanmar Companies Act that the Registerd Office of the Company is situated ad No.

SIGNATURE ....
(DIRECTOR)

Dated,   the   day of

DECLARATION OF OFFICIAL AND LEGAL VERSION

THE MYANMAR COMPANIES ACT 1913

AND

THE MYANMAR COMPANIES REGULATION N0-6

Name of the Company

Presented for filing by

To

Director General
Directorate of Investment and Company Administration Department
Ministry of National Planning and Economic Development
Office (32).Nay Pyi Taw.

I,

do hereby give you notice in accordance with Regulation No.6 of the Myanmar Companies Regulation 1957, that the official and legal version of the Company's Memorandum and Articles of Association and other documents shall be in English.

SIGNATURE ....
(DIRECTOR)

for and on behalf of
the Board of Directors

Nay Pyi Taw

the   day of

FORM XXVI

PARTICULARS OF DIRECTORS, MANAGERS AND MANAGING AGENTS AND OF ANY CHANGES THEREIN

(Myanmar Companies Act, See Section 87)

Name of Company :

Presented by :

The Present Christian name or names of surnames	Nationality, National Registration Card No.	Usual Residential Address	Other Business Occupation	Changes

NOTE :

(1) A complete list of the Directors or Managers or Managing Agents shown as existing in the last particulars.

(2) A note of the changes since the last list should be made in the column for " Changes" by placing against the new Director's name the word " in place of ...." and by writing against any former Director's name the word "dead " " resigned" or as the case may be giving the date of change against the entry

Dated this ....

Signature ....

Designation ....

THE MYANMAR COMPANIES ACT

PRIVATE COMPANY LIMITED BY SHARES

𝕸emorandum 𝕺f 𝕬ssociation

OF

COMPANY LIMITED

I.   The name of the Company is   COMPANY LIMITED.

II.   The registered office of the Company will be situated in the Union of Myanmar.

III.   The objects for which the Company is established are as on the next page.

IV.   The liability of the members is limited.

V   The authorised capital of the Company is Ks.   /- (Kyats Only) divided into (   ) shares of Ks.   /- (Kyats   Only) each, with power in General Meeting either to increase, reduce or alter such capital from time to time in accordance with the regulations of the Company and the legislative provisions for the time being in force in this behalf.

6. The Objective For Which The company is established are

7. To borrow money for the benefit of the Company's business from any person, firm,company, bank or financial organization in the manner that the Company shall think fit.

PROVISO: Provided that the Company shall not exercise any of the above objects whether in the Union of Myanmar or elsewhere,save in so for as it may be entitled so as to do in accordance with the Laws,Orders and Notifications in force from time to time and only subject to such permission and or approval as may be prescribed by the Laws, Orders and Notifications of the Union of Myanmar for the time being in force.

We, the several persons, whose names, nationalities, addresses and descriptions are subscribed below, are desirous of being formed into a Company in pursuance of this Memorandum of Association, and respectively agree to take the number of shares in the capital of the Company set opposite our respective names.

Sr. No:	Name, Address and Occupation of Subscribers	Nationality & N.R.C No.	Number of shares taken	Signatures

Yangon   Dated   the   day   of

It is hereby certified that the persons mentioned above put their signatures in my presence.

THE MYANMAR COMPANIES ACT

PRIVATE COMPANY LIMITED BY SHARES

𝕬𝖗𝖙𝖎𝖈𝖑𝖊𝖘   𝕺𝖋   𝕬𝖘𝖘𝖔𝖈𝖎𝖆𝖙𝖎𝖔𝖓

OF

COMPANY LIMITED

❖ ❖ ❖ ❖ ❖ ❖ ❖

1. The regulations contained in Table 'A' in the First Schedule to the Myanmar Companies Act shall apply to the Company save in so far as such regulations which are inconsistent with the following Articles. The compulsory regulations stipulated in Section 17 (2) of the Myanmar Companies Act shall always be deemed to apply to the Company.

PRIVATE COMPANY

2. The Company is to be a Private Company and accordingly following provisions shall have effect: -

(a) The mumber of the Company , exclusive of persons who are in the employment of the Company, shall be limited to fifty.

(b) Any invitation to the public to subscribe for any share or debenture or debenture stock of the Company is hereby prohibited.

CAPITAL AND SHARES

3. The authorised capital of the Company is Ks.   /- (Kyats
                            Only) divided into (   )
    shares of Ks.   /- (Kyats   Only) each,
    with power in General Meeting either to increase, reduce or alter such capital from time to time in accordance with the regulations of the Company and the legislative provisions for the time being in force in this behalf.

4. Subject to the provisions of the Myanmar Companies Act the shares shall be under the control of the Directors, who may allot or otherwise dispose of the same to such persons and on such terms and conditions as they may determine.

5.   The certificate of title to share shall be issued under the Seal of the Company, and signed by the General Manager or some other persons nominated by the Board of Directors. If the share certificate is defaced, lost or destroyed, it may be renewed on payment of such fee, if any, and on such terms, if any, as to evidence and indemnity as the Directors may think fit. The legal representative of a deceased member shall be recognised by the Directors.

6.   The Directors may, from time to time make call upon the members in respect of any money unpaid on their shares, and each member shall be liable to pay the amount of every call so made payable by instalments or may be revoked or postponed as the Directors may determine.

DIRECTORS

7.   Unless otherwise determined by a General Meeting the number of Directors shall not be less than (2) and more than (10).

    The First Directors shall be: -

    (1)
    (2)
    (3)
    (4)
    (5)

8.   The Directors may from time to time appoint one of their body to the office of the Managing Director for such terms and at such remuneration as they think fit and he shall have all the powers delegated to him by the Board of Directors from time to time.

9.   The qualification of a Director shall be the holding of at least (-) shares in the Company in his or her own name and it shall be his duty to comply with the provision of Section (85) of the Myanmar Companies Act.

10.   The Board of Directors may in their absolute and uncontrolled discretion refuse to register any proposed transfer of shares without assigning any reason.

PROCEEDINGS OF DIRECTORS

11.   The Director may meet together for the despatch of business, adjourn and otherwise regulate their meeting as they think fit and determine the quorum necessary for the transaction of business. Unless otherwise determined, two shall form a quorum. If any question arising at any meeting the Managing Director's decision shall be final. When any matter is put to a vote and if there shall be an equality of votes, the Chairman shall have a second or casting vote.

12.   Any Director may at any time summon a meeting of Directors.

13. A resolution in writing signed by all the Directors shall be as effective for all purposes as a resolution passed out at meeting of the Directors, duly called, held and constituted

POWERS AND DUTIES OF DIRECTORS

14. Without prejudice to the general power conferred by Regulation 71 of the Table "A" of the Myanmar Companies Act, it is hereby expressly declared that the Directors shall have the following powers, that is to say power:-

(1) To purchase or otherwise acquire for the Company any property, rights or privileges which the Company is authorized to acquire at such price, and generally on such terms and conditions as they think fit; also to sell, lease, abandon or otherwise deal with any property, rights or privileges to which the Company may be entitled, on such terms and conditions as they may think fit.

(2) To raise, borrow or secure the payment of such sum or sums in such manner and upon such terms and conditions in all respects as they think fit and in particular by the issue of debentures or debenture stocks of the Company charged upon all or any part of the property of the Company (both present and future) including its uncalled capital for the time being.

(3) At their discretion, to pay for any rights acquired or services rendered to the Company, either wholly or partially in cash or in shares, bonds, debentures or other securities of the Company and any such shares may be issued either as fully paid up or with such amount credited as paid up thereon as may be agreed upon; and any such bonds, debentures or other securities may be either specifically charged upon all or any part of the property of the Company and its uncalled capital or not so charged.

(4) To secure the fulfilment of any contract or engagement entered into by the Company by mortgage or charge upon all or any of the property of the Company and its uncalled capital for the time being or by granting calls on shares or in such manner as they may think fit.

(5) To appoint at their discretion, remove or suspend such Managers, Secretaries, Officers, Clerks, Agents and Servants for permanent, temporary or special services as they may from time to time think fit and to determine their duties and powers and fix their salaries or emoluments and to require security in such instances in such amount as they think fit and to depute any officers of the Company to do all or any of these things on their behalf.

(6) To appoint a Director as Managing Director, General Manager, Secretary or Departmental Manager in conjunction with his Directorship of the Company.

(7) To accept from any member on such terms and conditions as shall be agreed on the surrender of his shares or any part thereof.

(8)   To appoint any person or persons to accept and hold in trust for the Company any property belonging to the Company or in which it is interested or for any other purposes and to execute and do all such deeds and things as may be requisite in relation to any such trust.

(9)   To institute, conduct, defend of abandon any legal proceedings by or against the Company or its officers or otherwise concerning the affairs of the Company and also to compound and allow time for payment or satisfaction of any debts due to or of any claims and demands by or against the Company.

(10)   To refer claims and demands by or against the Company to arbitration and to observe and perform the awards.

(11)   To make and give receipts, releases and other discharges for money payable to the Company and for the claims and demands of the Company.

(12)   To act on behalf of the Company in all matters relating to bankruptcy and insolvency.

(13)   To determine who shall be entitled to sign bills of exchange, cheques, promissory notes, receipts, endorsements, releases, contracts and documents for or on behalf of the Company.

(14)   To invest, place on deposit and otherwise deal with any of the moneys of the Company not immediately required for the purpose thereof, upon securities or without securities and in such manners as the Directors may think fit, and from time to time vary or realize such investments.

(15)   To execute in the name and on behalf of the Company in favour of any Director or other person who may incur or be about to incur any personal liability for the benefit of the Company, such mortgages of the Company's property (present and future) as they think fit and any such mortgage may contain a power of sale and such other powers, covenants and provisions as shall be agreed on.

(16)   To give any officer or other person employed by the Company a commission on the profits of any particular business or transaction or a share in the general profit of the Company and such commission or share of profit shall be treated as part of the working expenses of the Company.

(17)   From time to time, to make, vary and repeal bye-laws for the regulation of the business of the Company, the officers and servants or the members of the Company or any section thereof.

(18)   To enter into all such negotiations and contracts and rescind and vary all such contracts and execute and do all such acts, deeds and things in the name and on behalf of the Company as they may consider expedient for or in relation to any of the matter aforesaid or otherwise for the purposes of the Company.

(19)   To borrow money for the benefit of the Company's business from any person, firm or company or bank or financial organization of local and abroad in the manner that the Directors shall think fit.

GENERAL MEETINGS

15   A general meeting shall be held within eighteen months from the date of its incorporation and thereafter at least once in every calendar year at such time (not being more than fifteen months after the holding of the last preceding general meeting) and places as may be fixed by the Board of Directors. No business shall be transacted at any general meeting unless a quorum of members is presented at the time when the meeting proceeds to business, save as herein otherwise provided Member holding not less than 50 percent of the issued shares capital (not less than two members) personally present, shall form a quorum for all purposes. And if and when in the case of there are only two number of members in the Company, those two members shall form a quorum.

DIVIDENDS

16.   The Company in general meeting may declare a dividend to be paid to the members, but no dividend shall exceed the amount recommended by the Directors. No dividends shall be paid otherwise than out of the profits of the year or any other undistributed profits.

OFFICE STAFF

17.   The Company shall maintain an office establishment and appoint a qualified person as General Manager and other qualified persons as office staffs. The remunerations and allowances such as salaries, travelling allowances and other expenditures incidental to the business shall be determined by the Board of Directors, and approved by the general meeting. The General Manager shall be responsible for the efficient operation of the office in every respect and shall be held accountable at all times to the Managing Director.

ACCOUNTS

18.   The Directors shall cause to be kept proper books of account with respect to:-
    (1)   all sums of money received and expended by the Company and the matters in respect of which the receipts and expenditures take place;
    (2)   all sales and purchases of goods by the Company;
    (3)   all assets and liabilities of the Company.

19.   The books of account shall be kept at the registered office of the Company or at such other place as the Directors shall think fit and shall be opened to inspection by the Directors during office hours.

AUDIT

20.   Auditors shall be appointed and their duties regulated in accordance with the provisions of the Myanmar Companies Act or any statutory modifications thereof for the time being in force.

NOTICE

21.   A notice may be given by the Company to any member either personally or sending it by post in a prepaid letter addressed to his registered address.

THE SEAL

22.   The Directors shall provide for the safe custody of the Seal, and the Seal shall never be used except by the authority of the Directors previously given, and in the presence of one Director at least, who shall sign every instrument to which the Seal is affixed.

INDEMNITY

23.   Subject to the provisions of Section 86 (C) of the Myanmar Companies Act and the existing laws, every Director, Auditor, Secretary or other officers of the Company shall be entitled to be indemnified by the Company against all costs, charges, losses, expenses and liabilities incurred by him in the execution and discharge of the duties or in relation thereto.

WINDING-UP

24.   Subject to the provisions contained in the Myanmar Companies Act and the statutory modification thereupon, the Company may be wound up voluntarily by the resolution of General Meeting.

❖   ❖   ❖   ❖

We, the several persons, whose names, nationalities, addresses and descriptions are subscribed below, are desirous of being formed into a Company in pursuance of this Articles of Association, and respectively agree to take the number of shares in the capital of the Company set opposite our respective names.

Sr. No:	Name, Address and Occupation of Subscribers	Nationality & N.R.C No.	Number of shares taken	Signatures

Yangon   Dated   the   day   of

It is hereby certified that the persons mentioned above put their signatures in my presence.

To:

The Director General

Directorate of Investment and Company Administration The Government of the Republic of the Union of Myanmar No. 1, Thitsar Road, Yankin Township, Yangon

Date:

Re: Intended Business Activities & Undertaking regarding trading activities

The intended business activities of the foreign company are as listed below
In English:
(i) ....
(ii) ....
(iii) ....
(iv) ....
(v) ....
(vi) ....
(vii) ....
(viii) ....

In Myanmar:
(i) ....
(ii) ....
(iii) ....
(iv) ....
(v) ....
(vi) ....
(vii) ....
(viii) ....

The applicant acknowledges that foreign companies are not allowed to conduct trading activities in Myanmar and undertakes not to conduct any trading activities.

....
Signature of proposed director

Name: ....

부록 5

Myanmar Special Economic Zones Law
The Pyidaungsu Hluttaw Law No. 1/2014
8th Waning of Pyatho, 1375 M.E
23rd January 2014

The Pyidaungsu Hluttaw hereby enacts this law

Chapter 1
Title, Application and Definition

1. This law shall be called the Myanmar Special Economic Zones Law.

2. This law shall apply to all Special Economic Zones.

3. The following expressions contained in this law shall have the meanings given hereunder
   (a) "State" means the Republic of the Union of Myanmar;
   (b) "Union Government" means the government of the Republic of the Union of Myanmar;
   (c) "Special economic zone" means a specified zone, notified and established as special economic zone under this law by the central body by demarcating the land area;
   (d) "Infrastructure" means tangible basic facilities such as electric power supply, water supply, waste water purification, roads, highways, railways, ports, airports, telecommunication networks, etc., and intangible facilities such as computer programmes and managerial arrangements for easy and effective operations;
   (e) "Developer" means a company, person or organization engaging, on a case-by -case basis with the permission of the management committee in accordance with the stipulations contained in this law, the rules, bye-laws, regulations and notifications issued under this law, in the construction, operation and

maintenance of the infrastructure of a special economic zone;

(f) "Investor" means a citizen, a foreigner or a joint venture established between a citizen and a foreigner who/that, on a case-by-case basis, has been granted permission by the relevant management committee to do business by investing in the special economic zone;

(g) "Citizen" includes also associated citizens and naturalized citizens. In this expression, economic organizations established exclusively by citizens are also included;

(h) "Foreigner" means a person who is not a citizen. In this expression, economic organizations established with foreigners [translator's note: i.e. not established exclusively by citizens] are also included;

(i) "Exempted zone" means a zone, specified by the relevant management committee and the customs department, that is regarded as if it were situated outside the country and in which customs duties and other taxes are, with regard to goods located in the special economic zone or transported into the special economic zone. In this zone, manufacturing, transportation and international wholesale trading may be conducted;

(j) "Promotion zones" means zones - which are not inland customs zones and exempted zones - for other businesses located in the special economic zone;

(k) "Exempted business" means an export-orientated business that is either (i) located in an exempted zone or (ii) outside an exempted zone or promotion zone, but has the right to enjoy the benefits available to a manufacturing business in an exempted zone;

(l) "Other business" means a business located either (i) in an area of the special economic zone which is not specified separately as exempted zone or promotion zone or (ii) in a promotion zone, but has [only] the right to enjoy the benefits available to an [ordinary] manufacturing business;

(m) "Other zone" means a zone specified by the Union Government from time to time, except high technology industrial zones, information technology zones, export-oriented production zones, port zones, logistics and transportation zones, science and technology research and development zones, services business zones, intermediary trading zones;

(n) "Central body" means the central body, formed by the Union Government under this law, for the administration of the special economic zones in Myanmar;

(o) "Central working body" means the central working body, formed by the central body under this law, in order to support the central body;

(p) "Management committee" means the management committee formed under this law to manage, administer and supervise the relevant special economic zone;

(q) "Responsible ministry" means the Union ministry charged by the Union Government with being responsible for implementing the necessary functions and duties under this law;

(r) "Assets" means land, buildings, vehicles, business-related capital, shares, promissory notes and similar instruments;

(s) "Profit accrued from assets" means a profit from the sale of assets, from mortgaging them, exchanging them or renting them out.

Chapter 2
Objectives

4. The objectives of this law are as follows

(a) To support the main goals of the national economic development project;

(b) To increase job opportunities for the people, to ameliorate their living standard, to promote the production of commodities, to increase export and to earn more income in foreign exchange;

(c) To encourage, promote and entice the harmonious development of the industry, economy and society;

(d) To promote industrial, economic and commercial enterprises, cooperation in services and finances between the state and other countries and to provide opportunities to citizens to learn vocational skills;

(e) To encourage and entice local and foreign investment by constructing infrastructure for developers and investors;

(f) To promote local and foreign investments in the special economic zones. To create new employment opportunities and to create industries next to the special economic zones.

Chapter 3
Formation of the Central Body and Functions and Duties thereof

5. The Union Government

(a) Shall, in order to implement the functions and duties contained in this law in respect of the establishment and operation of special economic zones, form a central body for the administration of the special economic zones in Myanmar, composed of a suitable person as chairman and suitable persons from the relevant ministries, government departments and organizations as members;

(b) Shall reconstitute the central body formed under sub-section (a) as necessary;

(c) Shall assign duties to the central body.

6. The functions and duties of the central body are as follows

(a) Laying down policies in order to implement the special economic zones successfully in accordance with the stipulations of this law and providing guidance as necessary;

(b) Reforming and establishing special high standard industry business, economic and commercial business, services, tourism, industry business based on agriculture, investment business, financial centres and centres for export-oriented industries in the selected regions in the country;

(c) Submitting the proposal to establish a special economic zone, which includes information as to the suitable place, required land area, extent of the land area and boundary demarcation, to the Union Government after having obtained and scrutinized the opinions of the relevant government departments and organizations;

(d) Forming the central working body and management committees with the approval of the Union Government to enable administration of the special economic zones, and assigning the functions and duties thereof;

(e) Laying down the arrangements and projects for the development and management of the special economic zones. Specifying work schemes and frameworks relating to implementation, surveillance and control;

(f) Scrutinizing and approving special economic zone development projects submitted by the management committees;

(g) Determining the categories of investment business and investment amounts in the special economic zones;

(h) Supervising the work of the management committees, inspecting them from time to time and communicating / coordinating with the relevant government departments and organizations;

(i) Granting, with the approval of the Union Government, relief from taxes and revenues, rental fees and land use premiums to be levied under this law;

(j) Increasing, with the approval of the Union Government, the tax exemption and relief periods in excess to those stipulated in this law in order to develop the whole country;

(k) Directing and supervising the "one-stop service" in the special economic zone in order to assure speed;

(l) Forming committees with the personnel of the relevant government departments and organizations in order to implement administrative, security, management and development matters in the special economic zones and determining the functions and duties of these committees;

(m) Requesting the management committees to supervise the committees formed under sub-section (l) directly;

(n) Reporting to the Union Government on the state of the implementation of the special economic zone projects;

(o) Establishing new special economic zones for the benefit of the country and the people. If industrial zones which are presently operational conform to the characteristics of specified special economic zones, upgrading such industrial zones to special economic zones with the approval of the Union Government and, thereafter, submitting the matter to the Pyitaungsu Hluttaw for approval;

(p) Performing other duties related to special economic zones as assigned by the Union Government.

Chapter 4
Formation of the Central Working Body and Functions and Duties Thereof

7. The central body shall, with the approval of the Union Government

    (a) in order to administer special economic zones, form a central working body, composed of relevant personnel from government departments and organizations;

(b) when forming the central working body according to sub-section (a), determine the duty of, and assign duty to, its chairman, vice-chairman, secretary and joint-secretary;

(c) reconstitute the central working body as necessary.

8. The functions and duties of the central working body are as follows –

(a) It shall scrutinize the proposals submitted by the management committees, developers or investors concerning special economic zones or investment businesses, and advise the central body;

(b) It shall scrutinize the special economic zone development projects submitted by the management committees and advise the central body;

(c) It shall scrutinize to determine the type of zone, the prioritized businesses, the types of business in accordance with the zone and submit the result to the central body;

(d) It shall study the matters related to international special economic zones and other special economic zones which should be implemented in Myanmar and their location, and advise the central body;

(e) It shall, with the approval of the central body and in accordance with the stipulations, coordinate with the relevant organizations in order to enable the investment businesses to be carried out in the relevant special economic zone;

(f) shall scrutinize other matters related to the administration, management and legal compliance of the investment businesses in the special economic zones;

(g) shall form, and assign duty to, other suitable working groups under the central body, if necessary.

Chapter 5
Formation of the Management Committees and Functions and Duties Thereof

9. The Central Body

(a) shall form, for each special economic zone, a management committee composed of personnel from relevant government departments and organizations, external personnel and personnel from external organizations in order to carry out the duties imposed by this law for the relevant special economic zone;

(b) shall include one representative of the relevant Region or State Government as member in the relevant management committee;

(c) shall, when forming a management committee according to sub-section (a), determine the chairman, the vice-chairman, the secretary and the joint-secretary;

(d) shall reconstitute the management committees as necessary.

10. The chairman of a management committee shall be responsible to the President of the Republic of the Union of Myanmar through the central body.

11. The functions and duties of the management committees are as follows

(a) submitting the special economic zone development project to the central body through the central working body and obtaining approval for the implementation and operation of the special economic zone;

(b) making arrangements so that investment businesses can be carried out in accordance with the stipulations;

(c) issuing permits to engage in an investment business within 30 days from the date of application, if the application includes all particulars stated in section 30;

(d) supervising and inspecting the implementation of the investment, land-use, environmental conservation, health, education, finance and taxation, development, transport, communication, security, electricity, energy and water supply, etc., and coordinating with the relevant government departments and organizations;

(e) coordinating with the relevant government departments and organization as may be necessary in order to protect the assets, profits and other rights of the investors in conformity with the existing laws;

(f) specifying, in notifications, orders, directives and procedures, the particulars to be followed by the investors;

(g) if the investors and their employees, their technicians, workers and family members are foreigners: coordinating with government departments and organizations in order to enable them to obtain entry visas and stay permits;

(h) coordinating matters with the Myanmar Central Bank to facilitate its financial management and supervision of foreign currencies and the financial business of investors in the special economic zone, and dealing with the banks permitted to do foreign banking business in Myanmar;

(i) permitting the developer, the investors, or the companies to carry out their business in the special economic zone in accordance with the stipulations, and supervising their performance;

(j) supplementing, amending and cancelling the rules pertaining to investments in the special economic zone from time to time, without affecting businesses that are already registered;

(k) demarcating the adjoining zones and locations in the special economic zone;

(l) offering a one-stop service: granting permits to invest in the special economic zone, registering companies, issuing entry visas for relevant jobs, issuing certificates of origin, taxation, issuing work permits and permissions to hire, issuing construction permits for factories and other investment and economic licenses;

(m) managing directly the departments established under the management committee in accordance with sub-section (l);

(n) scrutinizing whether the design and the construction of the special economic zone conform to the main plan;

(o) prescribing the particulars to be followed for the types of business that may be established in exempted zones and promotion zones, the minimum investment amount for each type of business, the minimum number of citizen employees to be hired, the standard norms for high technology;

(p) supervising environmental conservation and protection in the special economic zone in accordance with the existing laws, scrutinizing the system to dispose industrial waste from the factories, requesting developers and investors to comply with the stipulations;

(q) if necessary, forming a support committee, composed of representatives from relevant government departments or organizations, representatives of the developer and investors, and other suitable relevant personnel;

(r) in order to attract investment businesses, specifying and reforming, management patterns regarding the construction, operation and maintenance of the investment projects in the special economic zone, based on the advice of the support committee;

(s) issuing regulations to assure that the operation and management of the relevant special economic zone is one in compliance with the stipulations;

(t) granting exemptions and relief to investors or the developer in conformity with the Myanmar Special Economic Zones Law;

(u) carrying out the functions and duties specifically assigned to the management committee by the Union Government and the Central Body.

Chapter 6
Establishing a Special Economic Zone

12. The central body may, with the approval of the Union Government and after the matter has been submitted to, and confirmed by, the Pyidaungsu Hluttaw, establish a special economic zone in order to promote the development of the economy of the state, on the basis of the following criteria:

(a) international means of access such as ports, airports for easy communication between the international border and local markets;

(b) located in an area selected and prescribed by the Union Government for regional development;

(c) required infrastructure either already available or there are prospects that it will be built;

(d) Water resources and electric power available;

(e) adequate land available to establish industry and investment businesses;

(f) availability of skilled workers, semi-skilled workers and workers who can be trained; (g) possibility to implement training programmes to obtain required skilled workers;

(h) being a transportation hub.

13. If a plan to establish a special economic zone is feasible and beneficial to the state and the people, the central body may, with the approval of the Union Government and after having acquired the confirmation from the Pyidaungsu Hluttaw, establish the special economic zone, even if the criteria contained in section 12 are not met.

14. The central body

(a) shall select the developer through an open tender in accordance with the international procedures;

(b) shall give priority to a developer who is well experienced in the management of a special economic

zone and ensures benefits for the state and the people, prompt implementation of the project and transparency.

15. Foreigners may be allowed to own 100% of an investment business or to invest in a joint-venture a citizen.

Chapter 7
Prescriptions Related to Exempted Zones and Promotion Zones

16. The relevant management committee in a special economic zone

(a) may, as necessary, demarcate exempted zones and promotion zones;

(b) may demarcate other zones in addition to the exempted zones and the promotion zones according to market requirements;

(c) outside the demarcation of exempted zones and promotion zones, export-oriented businesses may be individually specified as an exempted zone.

17. Exempted businesses specified according to sub-section (c) of the section 16 shall enjoy the same benefits as businesses located in a demarcated exempted zone. Other businesses which are not specified as exempted may enjoy the same benefits as businesses located in a promotion zone.

18. The customs department

(a) shall ensure that goods imported into, or produced in, an exempted zone do not enter the country or a promotion zone without customs clearance;

(b) shall prescribe the methods of entrance into, and exit from, an exempted zone and the ways and means to be exercised in order to have secured fencing around the exempted zone so as to have security of the border;

(c) customs clearance in the special economic zone shall be carried out in accordance with customs procedures as they are practiced internationally. If it is deemed necessary, the customs department may carry out customs inspections in person at the location of the investor's business.

(d) if it is found that the investor is not in compliance with the stipulations, actions may be taken in accordance with the relevant customs procedures.

19. The customs department and the relevant departments shall specify the customs clearance procedures for transporting goods produced in an exempted zone to the local market or promotion zones.

20. Goods transported from an exempted zone to the local market or a promotion zone shall be regarded as imported materials goods. Raw materials imported into the exempted zone are to be manufactured into semi-finished or finished goods. If these goods are transported to the local market or a promotion zone, they shall be regarded as imported goods.

21. Unless there are specific stipulations to the contrary, customs duty and other relevant taxes shall be levied on the goods described in section 20 in accordance with the existing laws.

22. Goods transported from the local market or a promotion zone to an exempted zone shall be regarded as goods exported from the state.

23. Manufacturing businesses located in an exempted zone and exempted businesses shall primarily be export-orientated. In a special economic zone where exempted zones and promotion zones are not demarcated separately and supporting businesses exist, export- oriented businesses shall be specified as exempted businesses.

24. Businesses in an exempted zone may be 100% citizen-owned, 100% foreign-owned, or owned by a joint venture between citizens and foreigners.

25. The maximum percentage of goods produced in an exempted zone which may be transported to, and sold in, the local market or a promotion zone shall be stipulated in the rules.

26. When the goods are transported from the special economic zone to other countries, they shall be transported in sealed containers if they pass through the

external area of the special economic zone.

27. Businesses in a promotion zone may be 100% citizen-owned, 100% foreign-owned, or owned by a joint venture between citizens and foreigners.

28.

(a) A promotion zone is a place in the special economic zone based on the local market and may comprise manufacturing businesses, real estate businesses, department stores, banking businesses, insurance businesses, schools, hospitals, recreational facilities, etc., and investment areas.

(b) Goods manufactured in a promotion zone shall primarily be produced with local contents and directly transported and sold to businesses in an exempted zone.

(c) Other businesses which are not separately specified as exempted zone businesses or located in a promotion zone shall be regarded as investment business in a promotion zone.

Chapter 8
Investment Businesses; Duties of Investors; Exemptions Available

29. The investor shall have the right to do the following investment businesses in accordance with the stipulations in the special economic zones –

(a) manufacturing of finished products, manufacturing of processed goods, warehousing, transport, provision of services;

(b) importing the raw materials used in the investment, packaging materials, machinery, equipment, tools; transporting and importing fuel from domestic sources and overseas to the special economic zone;

(c) selling manufactured goods domestically or overseas in accordance with the stipulations;

(d) establishing and opening offices for the investment business and for overseas services with the approval of the management committee at the specified location in the special economic zone;

(e) engaging, with the approval of the management committee, in other economic businesses which are not forbidden by the state.

30. An investor desirous to engage in an investment business shall apply to the management committee in accordance with the stipulated rules and regulations in order to acquire an investment permit.

31. The investor shall complete the construction works and shall be able to commercially operate the investment business within the stipulated period. If the investor is not able to meet the deadlines, he must have good reason for it and report the reason to the management committee. If it is found that there is no good reason for the delay, the management committee may withdraw the investment permit in accordance with the regulations.

32. The investor shall have the right to enjoy the following income tax exemptions and reliefs −

    (a) Investment business an exempted zone or exempted business: Income tax exemption for the first 7 years from the date of commencement of commercial operations;

    (b) Investment business in a promotion zone or other businesses located in the special economic zone: Income tax exemption first 5 years from the date of commencement of commercial operations;

    (c) Investment business in an exempted zone or promoted zone: Reduction of the income tax rate by 50% for the second 5 years;

    (d) Investment business in an exempted zone or promotion zone: If profits, during the third 5 years, are re-invested within one year, 50% reduction of the income tax rate for profits derived from such re-investment.

33. If the exemption and relief periods contained in section 32 are not extended, the investor shall pay income tax in accordance with the stipulated rates as contained in the existing laws.

34. The investor −

    (a) shall register, with the DICA branch office which is to open jointly with the management committee, the business to be performed in the special economic zone and the company or organization in accordance with the stipulations;

(b) shall submit the status of the implementation of the investment business to the management committee in accordance with the stipulations;

(c) shall maintain and compile correctly the list of the businesses, the accounts and the documents in accordance with the international standards and norms;

(d) drugs and foodstuff that are damaged, of no use or not in conformity with the standards shall be destroyed at the specified location in accordance with the stipulations of the management committee.

35. The investor shall follow the standards and norms contained in the Myanmar Environmental Conservation Law and international standards and norms and must prevent social and health impacts in accordance with the existing laws.

36. If the investor wants to close or liquidate his business or organization, he must inform the relevant management committee in advance and shall carry out the closure or liquidation in accordance with the stipulations.

37. When the investor transfers some or all of the shares in his business, company or organization, he must inform the management committee in advance; the investment must be registered anew.

Chapter 9
Construction of a Special Economic Zone, Duties of the Developer; Exemptions Available

38. A special economic zone may be constructed as follows –

(a) The developer may be from the private sector, may be the government, or may be a joint venture between the private sector and the government;

(b) The developer may be 100% citizen-owned, 100% foreign-owned, a joint venture between citizens and/or foreigners and/or the government or between governments.

39. The developer –

(a) May conclude a land lease contract with the relevant management committee and, under the supervision of the management committee, construct the special economic zone, sub-lease land to the investors, and maintain the facilities of the special economic zone;

(b) The Union Government or the region or state government shall, in transparent procedures, establish the special economic zone, manage and maintain it either itself or entrust other organizations with it;

(c) Construction of each construction project shall be completed during the specified period. If the developer is unable to meet the deadlines, he shall have sound reasons for it and report the reasons to the management committee in advance. The land lease contract signed between the relevant committee and the developer shall be null and void if it is found that there is delay without sound reason;

(d) The developer may build the infrastructure in the special economic zone either himself or entrust the work to other organizations;

(e) Should the developer wish to invest in infrastructure outside the special economic zone which is connected to infrastructure inside the special economic zone, he may construct such infrastructure with the approval of the central board, but a separate investment vehicle has to be set up. Separate accounting shall be kept for each investment vehicle. The developer may, with the approval of the central body, enjoy similar benefits as a developer of a special economic zone. He may, for the construction of connected infrastructure such as roads, railways, bridges and water supply, enjoy further benefits with the approval of the central body if it takes considerable time to recover investments into such infrastructure;

(f) If connected infrastructure is to serve also areas outside the special economic zone in addition to areas inside the special economic zone, a contract for the provision of the external services shall be signed with the relevant government organizations in charge of the respective sector.

40. The developer shall be entitled to enjoy the following income tax exemptions and reliefs –

(a) Income tax exemption for the first 8 years from the commencement of commercial operations;

(b) 50% relief of the stipulated income tax rate in accordance with the existing laws for second 5 years;

(c) If profits, during the third 5 years, are re-invested within one year, 50% reduction of the income tax rate for profits derived from such re-investment.

41. If the exemption and relief periods contained in section 40 are not extended, the investor shall pay income tax in accordance with the stipulated rates as contained in the existing laws.

42. The developer may operate the infrastructure of the special economic zone himself or may sub-lease it to an investor for the permitted period or the period stipulated in the lease agreement with the management committee.

43. The developer shall pay the costs for the permitted land use and utility charges to the relevant management committee in accordance with the land lease contract, either by lump-sum payment or by payment in regular installments.

Chapter 10
Import Duty Exemption and Relief for the Developer and the Investors

44. Import duty exemption and relief shall be available as follows –

(a) Exemption from customs duty and other taxes, when the developer imports construction materials, machinery and equipment, heavy machineries, vehicles and materials used to construct the infrastructure and office rooms;

(b) Exemption from customs duty and other taxes, when the investor in an exempted zone imports raw materials, machinery, equipment and spare parts used in the production, and construction materials and vehicles used in the construction of the factories, warehouses and offices;

(c) Exemption from customs duty and other taxes, when the investor in an exempted zone imports motor vehicles and other goods for wholesale trading, export trading and logistic services;

(d) Exemption from customs duty and other taxes, or 50% relief from customs duty and other taxes for up to 5 years in a row, when the investor in a promotion zone imports machinery, equipment and required spare parts, construction materials for the factory, warehouses and offices, vehicles and other goods.

45. The investor in a promotion zone
(a) shall pay custom duty and other taxes regularly, when importing raw materials and other goods used for production;
(b) shall apply for reimbursement of the customs duty and other taxes which he paid when importing these materials, if the finished goods or semi-finished for the production of which the materials imported in accordance with sub-section (a) were used are exported or delivered into an exempted zone.

46. The developer and the investors −
(a) shall not be allowed to transfer and sell imported machinery, equipment and vehicles outside of the special economic zone;
(b) shall repay the amounts for which exemption or relief was obtained when importing the goods described in sub-section (a) are transferred and sold as a special case.

47. The developer and the investors shall request a decision of the relevant management committee concerning the temporary import period if machineries and equipment to be used in the initial construction work are to be imported short-term.

48. The developer and the investors in a special economic zone shall be allowed to carry forward, and set off, losses for 5 years from the year in which the loss was incurred.

49. Concerning commercial tax or value added tax −
(a) An exemption from commercial tax or value added tax may be granted to investors in an exempted zone;
(b) An exemption or relief from commercial tax or value added tax exemption may be granted to investors in a promotion zone during the relief period stipulated in this law. Commercial tax or value added tax shall be paid in

accordance with the relevant laws after the said relief period;

(c) An exemption from commercial tax or value added tax may be applied for by investors with regard to the export of goods manufactured;

(d) An exemption from commercial tax or value added tax may be applied for by investors in an exempted zone with regard to goods imported into the exempted zone from the inland or a promotion zone.

50. With the exception of goods prohibited or restricted by the Union Government, goods exported or re-exported from the special economic zone shall be exempted from tax and other direct or indirect levy.

51. The developer and the investors may apply for an exemption from income tax on each shareholder's share of the profit if dividends are paid from taxed income.

52. Investors in an exempted zone may be allowed to deduct, from the taxable income, expenditures actually incurred for training of skilled workers, unskilled workers, or management staff, or for research and development related to the investment project.

Chapter 11
Settlement of Disputes

53. If any dispute arises regarding the investment, this dispute shall be resolved amicably between the persons in disagreement.

54. If the settlement cannot be achieved under section 53

(a) the dispute shall be resolved in accordance with the agreed dispute resolution mechanism if the relevant contract contains provisions for the settlement of disputes;

(b) the dispute shall be resolved in accordance with the existing laws of the state if there is no provision for dispute settlement in the relevant contract.

Chapter 12
Taxes Payable by Deduction from the Source

55. If a foreigner, residing overseas, has not established and economic business in Myanmar, but is allowed to do business relating to a special economic zone in respect of any intellectual property right

(a) the payee shall make a deduction, from the amount payable to the concerned party as commission, interest, service fee, etc., in accordance with the stipulated income tax rate of the Income Tax Law;

(b) the payee shall make a deduction, from the amount payable to the concerned party as rental fee or similar other income, in accordance with the stipulated income tax rate of the Income Tax Law.

56. The relevant investor shall collect and pay, in accordance with the stipulated income tax rate of the Income Tax Law and in the currency prescribed by the central body, taxes on the income of the domestic and foreign employees and workers who are working in the special economic zone.

Chapter 13
Banks; Management of Finances; Insurance Business

57. Businesses operating in the special economic zone in a foreign currency shall have the right to open foreign accounts with any bank in Myanmar in possession of a banking operation license and receive and make payments in foreign currency in accordance with the stipulations.

58. The developer and the investors are entitled to exchange and transfer their own foreign currency within the special economic zone or overseas.

59. Local insurance companies, foreign insurance companies and insurance companies set up as a local/foreign joint venture shall have the right to operate their agency offices and insurance businesses within the special economic zones in accordance with the stipulations.

Chapter 14
Customs Management; Inspection of Goods by the Customs Department

60. Investors in an exempted zone and exempted businesses shall follow the rules, regulations and bye-laws, notifications, orders and directives issued under this law and according to this law. Investors in a promotion zone and other businesses shall follow the rules and regulations stipulated by the existing customs law.

61. The customs department shall reduce customs procedures and restrictions in exempted zones. It shall not engage in more control than is required to be in compliance with international agreements, maintain economical and social security and prevent illicit trading.

62. With regard to the transport of raw materials and equipment into exempted zones in order to manufacture goods for export, and the transport of exported goods to their overseas destination, customs declarations, the inspection of supporting documents, and, if necessary, the inspection of goods shall be done only in accordance with international practice.

63. The customs department shall use customs inspection methods in accordance with the customs procedures, but not engage in more inspections than are required based on the danger posed by the goods imported into the exempted zone.

64. The customs department shall speed up customs procedures by conducting, where required, inspections already on the premises of the investor. The customs officer shall seal inspected goods, if necessary, in order to prevent their loss in transport.

65. In order to offer smooth and convenient customs clearance, the customs department is entitled to delay inspections (of persons, ledger books maintained by the importer and exporter, records, work systems and trade data) until after a company directly or indirectly taking part in international trade has drawn the goods.

66. The trading of goods at a specified trading location in an exempted zone and

the display of goods in a trade exhibition shall be done in accordance with the customs procedures.

67. Regarding the transfer and transport of goods which are used in the manufacturing process in an exempted zone, the customs department may carry out inspections in accordance with the procedures.

68. The investor in an exempted zone may directly buy semi-finished goods from the inland or promotion zones in order to manufacture goods for export as well as required raw materials to be used in the export business, supplementary goods and packaging materials. The transport of the said goods into the exempted zone shall be done in accordance with customs clearance procedures.

Chapter 15
Quarantine Inspection and Confinement in Order to Prevent the Spread of Contagious Diseases

69. The responsible person from the quarantine department, directorate of health
   (a) shall, between the ports, airports and railway stations and the special economic zone, carry out quarantine inspections and confinement in order to prevent the spread of contagious diseases through transported goods, vehicles, containers, animals and plants which are to be directly imported to a special economic zone or transported from a special economic zone to the outside;
   (b) shall carry out, as may be necessary, quarantine inspections and confinement in order to prevent the spread of contagious diseases through the export or import items for the investment businesses within the special economic zone.

Chapter 16
Labour Matters

70. Concerning labour matters in the special economic zone, the management committee

(a) shall supervise the conclusion of employment agreements in accord with the stipulations;

(b) shall coordinate in order to determine the rights and duties of the employer and employee, or terms and conditions relating to employment contained in the employment agreement, so that employees can enjoy the benefit contained in the existing labour laws including minimum wages, leave, holiday, overtime pay, job loss allowance and workman's compensation;

(c) shall inspect and supervise so preserve the rights of the employees, technicians and staff;

(d) shall determine the minimum wages of employees and staff.

71. The investor may recruit freely through the employment and labour recruitment office, local recruitment agents or by own arrangement.

72. When employing skilled citizen workers, technicians and staff, the investor shall send, to the employee, the employment agreement mutually concluded between the employer and the employee in accordance with the existing labour law and rules.

73. The investor shall arrange for and provide necessary training in order to improve the skills of citizen employees and staff; the training is to be tailored to the types of work for which employees and staff are employed.

74. For work where expertise is not required, the investor shall hire citizens only.

75. Amongst skilled workers, technicians and staff, at least 25% must be citizens during the first two years from the commencement of commercial operations; at least 50% must be citizens during the second two years; and at least 75% must be citizens during the third two years.

76.

(a) The relevant management committee shall negotiate and mediate in the disputes arising between the employer and the employees, technicians or staff.

(b) If no settlement has been reached following negotiations and mediation by the relevant management committee according to sub-section (a), the parties shall accept the decision under the Trade Dispute Act of the Union of Myanmar.

77. The work permits for foreign employees who are working in the special economic zone shall be issued by the labour department representative office at the one stop service department in the special economic zone.

78. If an investor wishes to employ foreign employees for technology and management work in addition to the specified numbers, he may employ them with the approval of the relevant management committee.

Chapter 17
Land Use

79. The management committee may allow the developer or the investor to lease land or use land for up to 50 years upon payment of the land lease fee or land use fee. If the investor wishes to continue their business after the expiry of the term, the term may be extended for up to 25 years.

80. The developer or the investor
   (a) shall pay the agreed expenditures for transfer, resettlement and compensation if houses, buildings, gardens, paddy fields, fruit bearing plants and plantations on the land are required to be cleared or transferred;
   (b) shall, as necessary, negotiate with the management committee in order to ensure that the persons who have to leave the land do not fall below their previous standard of living, their fundamental needs are fulfilled and the transfer is easy and smooth;
   (c) shall use the permitted land in accordance with the prescribed regulations;
   (d) shall not be allowed to significantly modify or alter the topography or contour of the permitted land without the permission of the management committee;
   (e) shall report immediately to the management committee if natural mineral resources, antiques or treasures unrelated to the permitted business and not included in the original agreement are found above or under the land. If the

management committee so permits, the developer or investor may continue to operate on the land. Otherwise, the developer or investor shall transfer to a substituted area;

(f) shall rent out the land, permit the land use, or sell, mortgage, rent or give the land and the buildings to another person or another organization during the permitted period only with the approval of the management committee in accordance with the rules and regulations.

81. If the developer or the investor close the investment business or liquidate it, the land lease or the permit to use it shall be revoked, the land shall be returned and, if necessary, the buildings on the land shall be removed.

82. The Ministry of Home Affairs shall arrange for the confiscation or transfer of land that is located in the area where a special economic zone is specified and intended to be established by the central body in accordance with the existing laws.

Chapter 18
Miscellaneous

83. The assets, profits and other rights owned by the developer or investor shall be recognized and protected in accordance with the existing laws.

84. The price of the products, services or exported goods manufactured in an exempted zone or the promotion zone shall not be restricted and controlled.

85. The developer or the investor and their workers, technicians, employees and family members who are residing in the special economic zone shall follow the stipulations of this law in addition to other existing laws of Myanmar.

86. The investment businesses in the special economic zone are guaranteed not to be nationalized within the permitted period.

87. The relevant Union ministries and the region or state governments shall

implement the tasks pertaining to them contained in this law.

88. The persons assigned duty by the relevant Union ministry and the region or state overnments shall collect taxes and duties and fines recoverable under this law from the defaulter in accordance with the tax and revenue laws.

89. Notwithstanding anything contained in any existing law, the matters relating to any provision of this law shall be carried out only in accordance with this law.

90. The responsible ministry shall carry out the office work of the central body and bear the expenses.

91. The Union Government –
    (a) may assign duty the responsible ministry or any other ministry to carry out the office work of the central body and bear the expenses;
    (b) may, by notification, form any special committee, if it is necessary, from suitable persons to carry out the functions and duties of the central body;
    (c) may, by notification, form any management committee from suitable persons to perform manage ment and supervisory tasks;
    (d) may prescribe the functions and duties of the committees contained in sub-section (a) and (b).

92. Until the central body, the central working body and the management committees are set up under this law, the central body, the central working body and the management committees which were formed under the Myanmar Special Economic Zone Law (SLOR Law No. 8/2011), repealed by this law, shall be regarded as having been formed in accordance with this law.

93. The notifications, orders, directives and the procedures issued under the Myanmar Special Economic Zone Law (SLOR Law No. 8/2011), repealed by this law, shall continue to be valid as long as they are not contrary to this law.

94. The notifications, orders, directives and procedures issued by the central body, central working body and the relevant special economic zones management

committee shall not affect businesses that were registered before their issuance.

95. In implementing the provision contained in this law
  (a) The responsible ministry may, with the approval of the government, issue the required rules, regulations and bye-laws;
  (b) The central body, the central working body and the management committees may issue the required notification, order, directives and the procedures.

96. The Myanmar Special Economic Zones Law (SLOR Law No. 8/2011) and the Dawei Special Economic Zone Law (SLOR Law No. 17/2011) are revoked by this law.

....

I hereby sign according to the Constitution of the Republic of the Union of Myanmar.

(Sign) Thein Sein The President
The Republic of the Union of Myanmar

The State-owned Economic Enterprises Law
(The State Law and Order Restoration Council Law No. 9/89)
The 10th Waning Day of Tabaung, 1350 M.E (31st March, 1989)

The State Law and Order Restoration Council hereby enacts the following Law.

Chapter I
Title and Definition

1. The expression Government contained in this Law includes departments, corporations and other organizations under the Government.

2. This Law shall be called the State-owned Economic Enterprises Law.

Chapter II
Economic Enterprises to be carried out Solely by the Government

1. The Government has the sole right to carry out the following economic enterprises as State- owned economic enterprises:

1. Extraction of teak and sale of the same in the country and abroad;

2. Cultivation and conservation of forest plantation with the exception of village-owned fire-wood plantation cultivated by the villagers for their personal use;

3. Exploration, extraction and sale of petroleum and natural gas and production of products of the same;

4. Exploration and extraction of pearl, jade and precious stones and export of the same;

5. Breeding and production of fish and prawn in fisheries which have been reserved for research by the Government;

6. Postal and Telecommunications Service;

7. Air Transport Service and Railway Transport Service;

8. Banking Service and Insurance Service;

9. Broadcasting Service and Television Service;

10. Exploration and extraction of metals and export of the same;

11. Electricity Generating Services other than those permitted by law to private and co- operative electricity generating services;

12. Manufacture of products relating to security and defence which the Government has, from time to time, prescribed by notification.

2. The Government may, by notification, permit in the interest of the Union of Myanmar any economic enterprise which is prescribed under Section 3 to be operated solely by the Government to be carried out by joint-venture between the Government and any other person or any other economic organization or under conditions by any person or any economic organization subject to conditions.

3. The Government may, by notification, prohibit or prescribe conditions regarding the purchase, procurement, improvement, storage, possession, transport, sale and transfer of products derived from or produced by or used by economic enterprises which are prescribed under Section 3 to be carried out solely by the Government.

Chapter III
Right of carrying out other Economic Enterprises

1. Any person shall have the right to carry out any economic enterprise other than those prescribed under Section 3 to be carried out solely by the Government.

2. Without prejudice to the provision of Section 6, the Government may, in addition to those economic enterprises which are prescribed under Section 3 to be carried out solely by the Government, also carry out any other economic enterprise if it is considered necessary in the interest of the Union of Myanmar.

Chapter IV
Right to form Organizations

1. (a) In order to carry out the economic enterprises mentioned in Section 3 and

Section 7, the Government may, by notification:

1. Constitute organizations which are to undertake responsibility, and prescribe their duties and powers;

2. Re-constitute, if necessary, such organizations which are in existence at the time of the commencement of this Law, amend and prescribe their duties and powers;

3. Constitute one or more bodies to supervise the organizations mentioned in sub –sections and (2), if necessary, and prescribe their duties and powers.

(b) The respective organizations constituted under sub – section (a) shall be a body corporate having perpetual succession and a common seal, and shall have the right to sue and be sued in its corporate name.

Chapter V
Offences and Penalties

1. Whoever is convicted of an offence of carrying out, without the permission of the Government, any economic enterprise prescribed under Section 3 to be carried out solely by the Government shall be punished with imprisonment for a term which may extend to a period of 5 years and may also be liable to a fine. Furthermore, property both moveable and immoveable relating to the economic enterprise may be confiscated.

2. Whoever is convicted of an offence of violating an order or any condition notified under section 4 or section 5 shall be punished with imprisonment for a term which may extend to a period of 3 years and may also be liable to a fine.

Chapter VI
Miscellaneous

1. For the purpose of carrying out the provision of this Law, the Government may prescribe such procedures as may be necessary, and the respective Ministries may issue such orders and directives as may be necessary.

2. The Law conferring powers for Establishing the Socialist Economic System, 1965

is hereby repealed.

Sd./Saw Maung

General Chairman

The State Law and Order Restoration Council

미얀마 투자 법규 · 세무 가이드

초판 인쇄 2016년 6월 25일
초판 발행 2016년 6월 30일
—

지은이 이용태
펴낸이 이방원
—

펴낸곳 세창출판사
신고번호 제300-1990-63호
주소 03735 서울시 서대문구 경기대로 88 냉천빌딩 4층
전화 723-8660 **팩스** 720-4579
이메일 sc1992@empas.com
홈페이지 www.sechangpub.co.kr

ISBN 978-89-8411-616-0 93360

값 21,000원

이 도서의 국립중앙도서관 출판예정도서목록(CIP)은 서지정보유통지원시스템 홈페이지
(http://seoji.nl.go.kr)와 국가자료공동목록시스템(http://www.nl.go.kr/kolisnet)에서
이용하실 수 있습니다.(CIP제어번호: CIP2016014541)